The Artful Marketer

A Fundamental Business Guide for Creative Entrepreneurs

Minette Riordan, Ph.D.

The Artful Marketer

A Fundamental Business Guide for Creative Entrepreneurs
by Minette Riordan, Ph.D.

Cover Design by Melodye Hunter

Photo of Minette Riordan by R.S. Thurston Photography in
Santa Barbara, CA www.rsthurston.com

Copyright © 2014 by Minette Riordan, Ph. D.

The term ARTsignment™ is a trademark of Artella Creative
Mutlimedia, www.ArtellaLand.com

All rights reserved. No part of this publication may be
reproduced, distributed, or transmitted in any form or by any
means, including photocopying, recording, or other electronic
or mechanical methods, or by any information storage and
retrieval system, without the prior written permission of the
publisher and author, except in the case of brief quotations
embodied in critical reviews and certain other non-commercial
uses permitted by copyright law.

ISBN: 978-0-9909974-6-7 (p)
ISBN: 978-0-9909974-7-4 (e)

Crescendo Publishing, LLC
300 Carlsbad Village Drive
Ste. 108A, #443
Carlsbad, California 92008-2999

A Message from the Author

http://youtu.be/2CFRFwzY-uU

To help you implement the strategies mentioned in this book easily and get the most value out of the content, I've prepared some bonus materials I know you'll love. You can get instant access these complimentary materials at http://www.mindfulpatterns.com/artful-marketer-book

Praise for The Artful Marketer

Minette presents a very creative process for figuring out one of the toughest things for creative entrepreneurs...how to market themselves. Her fun and enjoyable way of dealing with some of the tough decisions demystifies the steps to connect with you ideal client in a way that they will say YES. If you're a creative entrepreneur, you'll actually enjoy the process of creating your marketing plan after reading this book.

~ Sharla Jacobs, Award-winning, Million Dollar Mentor to Coaches and Holistic Practitioners, Thrive Academy

If you are a creative entrepreneur who struggles with traditional types of linear planning or who fails to do any planning at all, then The Artful Marketer is the perfect book for you. Dr. Riordan provides all the fundamentals of building a 6-figure business, from a simple one-page business plan to a day-by-day marketing calendar that makes it easy to grow your business. Dr. Minette Riordan really does make marketing fun, creative and effective with her Color Wheel Marketing™ theory.

~ Patty Farmer, Business Growth Strategist, International Speaker, Radio Host & Best-selling Author

I am most heartened by the rise of "creative entre-preneurship" and the wider acceptance of the 'right-brained' way of thinking, especially coming from a family of artists and authors as I do.

It is interesting in light of my son's imminent foray into the world of community building and self-publishing as a fiction author, that so many of the things Minette talks about in her book, in terms of the attitudes towards the business aspects of the creative artist, have featured regularly in conversations with my son. He very much wants to be able to concentrate on the "art" of his business and not have to worry about the mechanics of promoting and selling products. If that is something that resonates with you as a creative looking to make money from their art then Minette's book is the book for you. Not only does it help enormously to know that it is perfectly okay to approach the business aspects of your creativity in the way that you do, but she also gives you plenty of right-brained tools and methods for making those aspects of your business work for you from that perspective. The opportunities to make a living from your art have never been so great and if this book encourages one person to do that then it has done its job! Here's to the success of all creative entrepreneurs!

~ Jasper Blake, Co-founder of Paycheck to Passion

I started reading your book yesterday evening and couldn't put it down until around 1:30 this morning. Girlfriend, you are reading my mail; writing my story; etc!!! I have an idea a minute all the time and have for years. I keep saying, I have no clue what I want to be when I grow up. I love the color wheel that you have created. Thank you, thank you, thank you for what you have created here for people like me and all of the other artsy-fartsy people in the world!

~ Peggy P. Edge, President Edge Packaging Systems

I was at a place in my business where I was feeling a little lost to my talents... Minette's book helped me see that even though I'm not an artist in a traditional sense... I am creative - and because of that a lot of traditional ways of running a business (marketing, bookkeeping) are not a perfect fit. I was feeling unbalanced - like I couldn't do a good job of "work" or life". Minette gives some solid strategies on how to blend life and work together - and how to truly honor your business - in a way that makes sense to creative entrepreneurs. If you are a creative thinker and know you need to focus more on running your business well in a way that doesn't feel like a strait jacket - this book is for you!

~ Meredith Eisenberg, Co-founder of Paycheck to Passion

The Artful Marketer: A Fundamental Business Guide for Creative Entrepreneurs brings shape, order and a plan to the business of growing a business. Minette Riordan draws on her experience as a business coach to share original and unique tools to make marketing more understandable, doable and fun! She enlightens and delivers! You will want to reread this and refer to it throughout your entrepreneurial journey. Learn how to put your creativity to work to help your business grow and flourish.

~ Deb Coman, Writing & Editing Professional,
www.debcoman.com

"The Artful Marketer" is a great resource for creative women entrepreneurs who cringe at the thought of marketing themselves. Read this book If you are ready to turn your ideas about marketing upside down! You will love the mindfulness tips, ARTsignments and journaling prompts. Well done!

~ Shann Vander Leek, Founder of Transformation Goddess

Finally: a business book for creative women entre-preneurs. If you worry about being "too salesy" or the idea of using a color wheel to develop your business plan captures your attention, then you'll want to read this book. A very nice balance between "how to" and "why to." Thanks.

~ Andrea Patten, Author of What Kids Need to Succeed,
www.andreapatten.com

The Artful Marketer is FINALLY addressing a critical missing piece for those of us who are creative entrepreneurs! To be able to end the struggles that most 'creatives' experience in building a business is such a relief. To be shown a way to become really successful, leveraging our own unique talents and abilities is both a gift and a blessing. The Artful Marketer may just be the answer to your prayers.

~ Wendy Darling, The Miracle Life Institute, Best-selling
Author of The Miracle That Is Your Life

Table of Contents

Dedication

To my wonderful husband, Brad Dobson, who has wholeheartedly supported me through all the ups and downs of my entrepreneurial journey. Thanks for your help, insight and patience in getting me through yet another creative project. I love you!

Chapter 1

Introduction

Welcome to *The Artful Marketer*. This book was written specifically to help creative women entrepreneurs like you attract more cash and clients. Why did I target creative women entrepreneurs? As a creative entrepreneur myself, I understand your pain and your challenges when it comes to marketing yourself. My mission is to help creative women entrepreneurs build profitable businesses that create the freedom, flexibility, and financial independence they dream of.

Current statistics show that there are close to 10 million women-owned businesses, but on average, women-owned businesses don't have a high rate of success. Did you know that of those 10 million businesses, only 6 percent will ever reach the six-figure mark? Even sadder, only 2 percent of women-owned businesses ever reach the seven-figure mark. In fact, over 50 percent of women never exceed $25,000 dollars a year in revenue. It doesn't have to be that way.

I would like to turn these statistics upside down and see more and more women entrepreneurs break through to their first $50,000, $100,000 and yes, even 1 million in revenue in their business. I believe that the number one reason that creative women entrepreneurs in particular are not succeeding in their businesses is that they don't know how (and perhaps are afraid) to market themselves. The second reason that creative women entrepreneurs fail to meet their financial goals is that they avoid, ignore, or are numb to their numbers.

This book will show you why you must learn to love your numbers and how to do that in a way that is creative, playful, and simple. It will also show you how to shift your mindset around marketing so that marketing becomes meaningful, creative and, most importantly, effective. The combination of mindset, money, and marketing is the secret to attracting cash and clients—fast. I guarantee to make this process fun. And I guarantee that if you do the work and follow the plans that I have created for you, you will get results.

What is a Creative Entrepreneur?

I would define a creative entrepreneur as someone who sees her creativity as the core of the work she does in the world. You might be an artist, writer, speaker, coach, graphic designer, interior designer, blogger, massage therapist, healer, or any of a number of other careers that are labeled as "creative" or "artistic." You could work in any of these industries and not be an entrepreneur. An entrepreneur has a certain mindset that is distinct from that of a business owner or an employee. Simply defined, an entrepreneur is a person who solves problems for other people at a profit. This is your first mindset shift. No matter what type of product or service you are selling, you have to understand what problems it solves for a specific group of people. I will go into this mindset shift in much greater detail later in the book.

What makes a creative entrepreneur different from any other woman entrepreneur? Take a look at the following checklist. If you agree with three or more of the statements in this list, you are a creative entrepreneur.

- I am a visual or kinesthetic learner.
- I consider myself to be right-brained.
- I am always so full of ideas I feel like I can barely contain them.
- I can see connections between people or ideas that other people don't see.
- I consider myself to be highly creative in my work and in my life.
- I am passionate about what I do.
- I am not a linear thinker. I struggle with structure and systems.
- I prefer to work alone or with a collaborative team.

- I love to go with the flow and not follow a rigid schedule.
- I find certain aspects of building a business—like creating a budget or selling my services—to be frustrating.
- I am easily overwhelmed by too many details.

How many of these statements did you agree with? I could answer "Yes!" to every sentence on the list. I can see my gifts and my challenges as a creative entrepreneur for the past fifteen years mirrored in these statements. Hindsight is always 20/20, isn't it? I wish I had understood this about myself when I started my first business in 2001.

How Creative Entrepreneurs Feel about Marketing

It wasn't until I started my coaching business in 2013 that I began to get a clear picture of who the creative entrepreneur is and to understand her unique challenges and amazing gifts. As I struggled to identify who I wanted to be as a coach and to avoid the massive mistakes that I made in my first business, I started to see myself reflected in my creative clients. A very clear picture of the creative entrepreneur started to emerge. The creative women entrepreneurs I worked with shared several common beliefs about their ability to build a profitable business, and you will hear their personal stories throughout this book. Here are some of the comments they have shared with me:

- Marketing is so overwhelming; I don't know where to start.
- I'm afraid to sell myself; people will think I'm pushy.
- If I start marketing all the time, no one will want to be my friend on Facebook.
- Creating a marketing plan feels like pulling teeth; it's not fun or creative, so I just wing it.
- Can't I just use social media to grow my business?
- I'm not good at technology.
- Networking terrifies me—I'm such an introvert.
- Networking is fun. I love being around people, but I never get any business out of it, so I stopped going.
- I'm not a marketer; I just love to _____ (fill in the blank).
- I'm terrible at marketing; it feels so unnatural, so I don't do it.
- I don't have time for marketing; my day is already so busy.

Do some of these statements resonate with you? If so, then this book is written for you! I want to change your mindset about marketing, and I want to make marketing both fun and meaningful for you. The sooner you learn how to be an effective and heart-centered marketer, the sooner the cash and clients will flow in.

I loved this description of marketing from Ryan Eliason.

He writes:

> I invite you to consider the possibility that marketing and sales may be one of the most important skills you need to develop if you want to explode your positive impact, and manifest your higher purpose and mission.
>
> Fortunately, I believe that marketing can be done with love and integrity. It can be transformed from being simply a means to an end, into being an authentic and central activity to accomplish your purpose and mission. It can be one of the ways you spread a positive message and build your movement. It can ultimately become one of the primary ways that you connect with and serve people that you love.
>
> What could be more satisfying than that?

The creative women entrepreneurs I work with see their work in the world as bigger than themselves. They are not trying to create a job for themselves. Rather, they want to support and nourish a lifestyle that allows them the freedom and flexibility to pursue their dreams. They are big dreamers with huge hearts and a clear vision of what they want to accomplish. Many of them want to create movements and change the world, one person at a time. All of them are visionary and visual thinkers. Once I understood this about creative women entrepreneurs and about myself, I knew I needed to shift how I was teaching marketing.

How Creative Entrepreneurs Learn

According to Time4Learning.com:

> **Right brained, visual learners tend to have several things in common.** They visualize images in their brain and can have long-term memory of these images. They don't usually perform well on sequential, or linear tasks (such as following multi-step instructions). They learn information in chunks, in a holistic way. They learn much better by demonstration than by explanation. And they are naturally creative problem solvers.

When most of us were in elementary school, teachers tended to address different learning styles and to approach teaching using a broad variety of visual, audio, and tactile aids to appeal to the multiple learning styles in the classroom. Sadly, that variety of teaching styles does not extend to the boardroom or the business-planning seminar. Creative women entrepreneurs get stuck in their business because traditional methods of planning don't work for them. Marketing plans, strategies, and tactics are usually presented with too many details, too much structure, and without enough color or meaning for the creative entrepreneur.

Yet, in recent years there has been a surge in the number of creative methods used for teaching as well as for creative problem solving inside companies and among entrepreneurs. Creativity is the hottest new trend in business. If you do a search for creativity in business, you might be surprised to find that there is a whole movement to bring more creativity into the workplace. Yes, I know, you are already wholeheartedly embracing creativity as a way of life, but did you know that you can use your natural creativity to plan, design, and implement your marketing strategy?

One of my favorite methods for creative planning that has achieved recent popularity is visual mapping—using wall-sized sheets of paper covered in cartoons, doodles, and words. In fact, the doodling craze is in full swing today as witnessed by the popularity of books such as *The Doodling Revolution* by Sunnie Brown and the international art craze called Zentangle®. Just go to Amazon and search for "doodling" to see the variety of inspirational books and ideas. I also know that mind maps and colorful flow charts can be great planning tools for creative people.

In this book I will be introducing my own visual marketing plan system based on the color wheel. Get ready to dust off the markers, let the crayons out of the box, and discover how to approach marketing from a playful and soulful perspective. There are a few supplies I would encourage you to have on hand as we begin this journey together. Here is a list of suggested supplies to have on hand:

- Blank journal or paper
- Pens, markers, crayons, colored pencils
- Scissors
- Glue
- Tape
- Old Magazines
- Sticky Notes
- Poster Board(s)

Why Is Creativity Such a Hot Topic in Business Today?

Authors such as Seth Godin, who is one of my favorite marketing mentors, are touting creativity as an invaluable skill in business. In his insightful book *The Icarus Deception*, Godin claims that we are all artists; we must see our work as art, no matter what industry we are in. The book goes on to discuss why creativity is the wave of the future in business. Godin also understands why creative entrepreneurs struggle to be successful. "99% of the time, in my experience, the hard part about creativity isn't coming up with something no one has ever thought of before. The hard part is actually executing the thing you've thought of." I have seen this happen over and over again with my clients, lots of ideas but no follow-through, no plan, no profit.

Creativity is crucial to success, but so is action.

Linda Naiman, founder of Creativityatwork.com, writes:

> Creativity is the act of turning new and imaginative ideas into reality. Creativity is characterized by the ability to perceive the world in new ways, to find hidden patterns, to make connections between seemingly unrelated phenomena, and to generate solutions. Creativity involves two processes: thinking, then producing. If you have ideas, but don't act on them, you are imaginative but not creative.

That last line, about having ideas but not acting on them, is true of many of the creative entrepreneurs I work with. Creative women entrepreneurs love the creative aspects of the work they do—they love brainstorming and the free flow of ideas—but they don't always know how to take an idea and create an action plan that will help them go from idea to profit. Marketing is the key ingredient to making a profit from your ideas. At the end of this book, you will find a chapter written by my husband that talks about how to support a creative entrepreneur. One of our biggest challenges is our love of chasing new ideas!

In the following pages, you will find the support you need to take any idea and learn how to monetize it by putting a simple, one-page plan in place.

Business Lessons from Buddha

> *"Meditate. Live purely. Be quiet. Do your work with mastery. Like the moon, come out from behind the clouds! Shine."* – Buddha

I owned a publishing company for eleven years. When I started my parenting magazine in 2001, I agonized over every detail and every word. I cringed each time a new issue came out, knowing there would be the inevitable mistake. Over time, I learned to be at peace with the product. I did my best, had great editors, and worked hard to make sure all the ads were correct, even if a few of the articles had an occasional typo. I learned to relax into the process of getting things going rather than getting them right.

Then I started to make art again ... and the voice of my inner critic rang out loud and clear. I have been reluctant to paint anything representational. I was playing it safe with my doodling and coloring books. *I can't draw*, I said to myself. *And draw a face? Really?* Part of my ongoing success in business stems from my willingness to confront my inner critic, to ask her to take a hike and let me play.

I find that spending time in my craft leaves me feeling fresh and inspired to take new actions in my business when Monday morning rolls around! It takes me outside my normal routine and gets me away from the computer. Working on creative projects on the weekends inspires wonderful new ideas for blogging, or for programs and projects I want to work on like writing this book. I would encourage you to look for creative ways to bring more play into your business planning. I will be sharing ideas throughout the book, but you know how your brain works better than anyone else. Allow your inner teacher to guide you on this journey.

The quote from Buddha at the beginning of this section reminds me to look at ways to integrate my business passion with my creative calling: meditate, live purely, be quiet, do my work with mastery, and be willing to shine.

Rediscovering my creative spirit has taught me to stretch and to focus at the same time. It has reminded me of that gentle path that Buddha defines as the path of right action. Doing my work with mastery has helped me finish projects and pick one idea or project at a time to carry through to completion. I have crossed over from simply being imaginative to being creative, as Linda Naiman reminds us in her definition of creativity.

For me, creating art is a form of meditation that inspires deeper reflection and leads me on a merry journey of inner exploration. Yet at the end of the day, it takes courage and confidence to share what I create in my craft room on my blog or social media channels. That inner critic still rears her ugly head and tries to stop me from letting my light shine.

The Buddha reminds us to come out from behind the clouds and shine! To me, that means bringing all of who we are to the work that we do, to be willing to stand in the moonlight and say, "Here I am!" When you master the ability to shine, the people who have been waiting for you will show up.

I find that my clients struggle mightily with standing up and allowing the light to shine on them. They struggle with asking for what they need. They struggle with putting themselves out into the world in a way that says, "Here I am, look at me!" I want all creative women entrepreneurs to give themselves permission to shine their gifts out into the world so that they can attract money, clients, fame, freedom, adventure. I am going to teach you how to do this in a way that fulfills you and in a way that is meaningful and allows you to serve more and more people.

At the end of the journey, you will have a new perspective on what marketing means to you, and you will have a plan in place that will make it easy for you to attract all the cash and clients you want—fast!

Creating Mindful Patterns

The key to marketing success is consistency and persistence.

In June of 2014, I traveled to Providence, Rhode Island, to become certified as a Zentangle® teacher. I didn't go with the intention of wanting to teach the Zentangle® process, which is a meditative form of drawing. I went to deepen my own practice and experience with tangling. I stumbled across a reference to Zentangle® on a friend's blog about four years ago, and I think I surprised myself when I stuck with it. As a creative entrepreneur, I love bright, shiny new classes, tools, and techniques. My love of learning gets me into trouble sometimes. Instead of sitting down and taking action on what I already know, I go learn something new. This is true in my business as well as my personal life. I love input, which often sparks a flood of new ideas. Suddenly I am back in the place of imagination, following a dream down a path but (not?) getting all the way to the treasure at the end.

The meditative format of the Zentangle® process has reminded me of the value of several things: taking my time, breathing and focusing on the task at hand. Practice is essential when trying out a new pattern. Sometimes it takes multiple tries to get a new pattern just right. When I try to rush a pattern, my lines are uneven, my circles aren't round, and I am not pleased with the results.

Marketing requires these same skills: focus, taking your time, breathing, and practice. In the past few months, I found myself chasing another bright, shiny idea down the rabbit hole. I was contemplating launching a new website focusing on Zentangle® and the art of business. I wanted a place where people could gather to learn the Zentangle® process, but I also wanted to build a community to support all the CZTs (Certified Zentangle Teachers) who are trying to grow their business.

My husband, Brad, and I love to walk together in the mornings and often use this time to brainstorm about what we want to create or do. I was telling him about my idea for this website but was stumbling to find the right name. I described to him what I wanted to create, and he said he needed to think about it. Brad came back to me later in the day and said, "How about Mindful Patterns?"

In that moment, my heart expanded and so did my vision of what this website would become. Suddenly it did not seem so simple. As I began to sift through ideas, to dream and to try to organize what I wanted to create, I realized that Mindful Patterns are what I teach my clients to create in their business and in their lives. I encourage my clients to journal, to be creative, and to use their artistic talents to help them plan. I also encourage them to engage in the practice of mindfulness. What is mindfulness? I like this definition:

Mindfulness means maintaining a moment-by-moment awareness of our thoughts, feelings, bodily sensations, and surrounding environment.

Mindfulness also involves acceptance, meaning that we pay attention to our thoughts and feelings without judging them—without believing, for instance, that there's a "right" or "wrong" way to think or feel in a given moment. When we practice mindfulness, our thoughts tune into what we're sensing in the present moment rather than rehashing the past or imagining the future.

Mindfulness is an essential element of success, especially for creative entrepreneurs whose minds are often on overdrive. Mindfulness reminds us to stay present, connected, and focused. Marketing is all about discovering the mindful patterns that work for you. It takes persistence and consistency to successfully build a business. But it also takes mindfulness. I realized that this idea of Mindful Patterns encompasses all aspects of the creative entrepreneur's gifts and challenges. Together Brad and I realized that Mindful Patterns is also the name of the company that we are building. This book is the first in the Mindful Patterns publishing series.

Throughout this book you will find quotes and ideas for creating Mindful Patterns in your life and in your business. If there is one thing that I know for certain about creative women entrepreneurs, it's that there is little or no separation between our work and our lives. In fact, it's the ability to have the freedom and flexibility to create a meaningful lifestyle while doing work we are passionate about that called us to become entrepreneurs. Now it's time to learn how to profit from that passion, without sacrificing more time and energy.

Creative Toolbox

In the following chapters, I will share a variety of Mindfulnes Tips, ARTsignments™ and Journaling Prompts. The intention of these activities is to provide you with ideas and tools for thinking about marketing from a new perspective. Marketing can be creative and fun when approached with the right mindset. The types of activities are outlined below. Each activity has it's own symbol.

 Mindfulness Tips – suggestions for connecting to self and Spirit

 ARTsignments™ - an art project that is designed to activate and expand self-awareness and transformation, guiding you to look at your business from a different angle than you have appreciated before

 Journaling Prompts – questions, fill-in-the-blank sentences and prompts to inspire your creative thinking

Chapter 2

Riding the Money Roller Coaster

In 2001, my children were three and one, and I was going stir crazy. I realized that I was not cut out to be a stay-at-home mom. Don't get me wrong—I adore my kids, who are now fifteen and thirteen, but I was unhappy and driving my family crazy.

I have a doctorate from Stanford in Spanish, I specialized in twentieth-century Latin American poetry, and I thought I was going to be a college professor. Instead, my path took me to Redding, California, where I taught at a private boarding school for troubled teens for a couple years before starting my family. I loved working with that population, and boy! did they ever teach me about what it means to be authentic and to walk your talk! After a few years, we followed my husband's work to Plano, Texas.

I knew I didn't want to go back to teaching full-time. I wanted the best of both worlds: a business that kept me intellectually stimulated and provided a flexible schedule so that I didn't have to put my kids in daycare full-time. My husband and I have always been very clear about our parenting values and how we wanted to raise our kids.

So I decided to launch a parenting magazine in my community. I knew nothing about the publishing industry, media, or marketing; I just thought it would be fun. How hard could it be?

I dove right in, started selling ads, and turned a profit with my very first issue. It was pretty exciting. In the beginning, I published only four times a year, leaving lots of time between issues for family and volunteer activities. I took my kids everywhere. Since most of my clients worked with kids or had children of their own, we would often meet at a Starbucks or McDonald's PlayPlace with our kids in tow.

As businesses often do, this one started to take on a life of its own. It grew from a small quarterly publication with a print run of 20,000 magazines distributed around my county to a monthly magazine with over 50,000 copies being distributed across the Dallas/ Ft. Worth Metroplex. Suddenly my little business turned into a rolling stone, and I often found myself chasing the business rather than leading it. I had to learn how to lead others as the business grew, and I acquired an office, a staff, and various vendors to help with the distribution. I can't say that I always handled leadership gracefully, and I learned many lessons about myself in the process.

One of the many mistakes that I made was to not have a clear goal of where I was headed with my business. I didn't have financial goals, but I also didn't have a plan in place for strategically moving forward, growing, and continuing to love my business. In formal business terms, I didn't have a business plan or an exit strategy. I just started working and kept going. My office manager said one time that it felt like we were digging a ditch. We had our heads down and were working hard, tossing shovelfuls of dirt out of our way. But we didn't know why we were digging the ditch or which direction it should go.

By year three, the business was bringing in over six figures. We were able to maintain that level of income for several years, but during that time, I made one major mistake. The sad thing is, I didn't even know it was a mistake. I didn't start this business to make money. I thought I did, but the truth is I was so focused on the creative and social aspects that I failed to pay close enough attention to the financial details. I always thought I wasn't any good at money.

I would hire people without really understanding if I could afford them. I would have faith that they would return my investment in them by increasing our advertising sales. Then it would turn out they couldn't sell advertising, or they discovered they really didn't want to. But that wasn't my biggest mistake.

My biggest mistake was that I never paid myself a salary.

No one told me—and I didn't know to ask—that paying yourself a salary from your business is really important for two reasons.

The first reason is financial: if you ever plan to sell your business, owner salary is one of the key pieces of valuing your company. Because I didn't show profit or pay myself, my company wasn't worth much, even when it was grossing hundreds of thousands of dollars.

The second reason is more personal: when you pay yourself a salary, it shows that you are treating your business like a business. I was treating my business like a very expensive hobby.

Treat Your Business Like a Business

Start a plan for paying yourself, even if it is only $25 a week. Write your plan in your journal and for every week that you transfer money, celebrate! Give yourself a gold star or draw a smiley face. If you are treating your business like a business, you will have a personal checking account as well as a business one. Transfer cash from your business account to your personal account every week. It's not about the amount;

it's about the habit and the mindset. Use your journal to support your progress.

When the economy crashed in 2008, my business went downhill quickly. Many of our clients were afraid to spend money, and 30 percent of them went out of business completely. Our revenue dropped dramatically. We made cuts where we could and made some changes to our business model, but it was a very stressful year. By this time I was starting to feel ashamed of my business and myself because I couldn't figure out how to make money.

Issues around money have always made me feel a bit queasy. In college I tended to run up credit card debt I couldn't pay off. Again, I wasn't paying attention to the details of how money works. I wanted something and I would buy it. I worked hard and made good money, but I didn't understand how to manage my cash flow even then. Sometimes I would have to call my stepdad and ask to borrow money to pay off debt. Ugh. That was never fun. He was always generous and I always paid him back, but asking was hard.

That fear of asking for money impacted my business when I needed to call to negotiate with a vendor or remind a client their payment was due. Some of my bad personal money habits definitely followed me into my business. Suddenly, I had accumulated over $50,000 in debt, and I didn't know what to do, but I learned.

I learned what numbers I needed to be paying attention to on a weekly and monthly basis. I managed my sales and revenue better. We continued to make cuts in our costs and to scale back on production, and we successfully paid down our debt every month. I even took back the design of the magazine and started doing the layout myself again so that I could save that money.

We were limping along when suddenly, I had one of the most bizarre days I had ever experienced in my business. It was August of 2009. My family and I had just returned from a two-week vacation in Nova Scotia, relaxed and happy. My office manager did a great job of keeping everything going while I was gone. She was incredibly competent and supportive.

I discovered the morning I returned to the office that she had waited for me to get back from vacation to tell me that we didn't have enough cash in our bank account to pay our staff. As usual, we had $20,000 to $30,000 dollars in outstanding invoices. She had been working hard to collect this money, but times were still challenging, and so many of our small business clients were struggling to keep their doors open.

My stomach dropped, that awful queasy feeling overwhelmed me, and I had no clue what to do in that moment. I just felt afraid and sick.

While I was gone, my office manager told me that someone from our local chamber of commerce wanted to meet with me and kept asking when I would return from vacation. When I arrived at the office that first day back, I was in a pair of shorts and a T-shirt. I had not done my hair, and I had no makeup on. I'm sure I was pale after the announcement about the money.

My office manager and another staff member were scurrying around trying to straighten up the office, and I could not figure out what was going on. My office was in the back of the building, and I could hear them moving around, but I was more worried about trying to come up with the $5,000 I needed that day to make payroll.

My husband and I didn't have any savings at the time and had already put so much into the business. At that moment, I felt overwhelmed, and I certainly didn't feel like a successful business owner.

Suddenly I heard the front doorbell ring, and a flood of people poured into the office. My office manager asked me to come to the conference room. Here I was, dressed like a bum and feeling pretty out of sorts. I walked into a conference room full of friends and colleagues from our local chamber of commerce.

It turned out I had just been named the Small Business Owner of the Year. They were waiting for me to get back from vacation so that they could tell me personally before announcing it publicly.

All I can remember about that moment is feeling ashamed and like a failure. I didn't deserve this award. How could I when I couldn't even pay my bills? I couldn't look back at all the contributions I had made to my community and to my local chamber of commerce. I couldn't see how successful I had been in so many ways. All I could see was that I was not a good business owner, and I didn't deserve this award.

Even a month later when I had to accept the award publicly and got to meet the governor of the state of Texas, I still felt raw inside. The award seemed to highlight my inability to build a financially profitable business.

But that was not to be the end of that crazy roller-coaster day. A few hours after the chamber group left, I did what I have always done. I figured out where to get the money. We had to borrow it from a personal credit card. It was pretty much the last credit we had left—personally or in our business. But at least I could breathe, knowing my people were getting paid. I could see all that money sitting in our receivables, but I couldn't make people pay me any faster. The immediate crisis was solved, but there were definitely some bigger issues to deal with, and I was still afraid of what might happen.

I was also desperately afraid that word would get out that I was a fraud and a failure. As I sat at my desk thinking about all of this, I received a call from a company who was interested in buying my magazine.

Could this day get any weirder? What was the universe trying to tell me? My emotions were a total wreck, but could selling the magazine be an option and my salvation?

It wasn't the first time we had talked about selling or even shutting down the business, but we were stuck in an office lease for another eighteen months. To break the lease would cost thousands of dollars we didn't have, not to mention the rest of the debt we were trying to pay off.

I had a great conversation with a publisher about our magazine and whether it was a match for the publishing company that he was building. I got all my financials together and sent them off to him for review.

At the end of the day, he opted not to buy my business. I was still in the same dire straits, but I had hope. In hindsight, not getting off lightly by selling my business was a good thing. I had to figure it out on my own.

Over the next couple years, we continued to plug along, pay down our debt, and try new ways to make enough money. Eventually, my husband and I realized that this business and our lifestyle were not at all what we wanted for ourselves or for our kids. My kids were spending more time at the office than at home.

It was time for a dramatic life makeover. I ended up converting my print magazine to an online magazine, finding someone to sublease the office, and moving my business back home where it started. I found someone who wanted to take over the business, and she spent a year training with me. My husband and I made a commitment to leave Plano, Texas, in the summer of 2012 and relocate to Santa Barbara, California.

We had no idea how we were going to afford it or if it was even possible, but we made it happen. We started saving money, paid off personal debt, and put plans in place to sell our home in Texas. We were committed to moving to California, no matter what it might look like on the other end—new jobs, living in a small apartment with two teens—we didn't care. We knew we had to go.

Because we were so committed to making this happen no matter what it might look like, everything that could go right did. My friend took over my business; I sold it to her for $100. At that point, I just wanted out and I didn't care about the money. I was done. Combining the sale of our house with our savings, we easily had enough money to make the move. An uncle gave us the down payment for a house, and my husband kept his job and now works from home, which has always been his dream. We share an office and are both present almost every day when the kids come home from school.

And me? I spent the past two years making peace with myself and launching a new business that I love. I have learned that I am good at money. I am great at supporting others in making their dreams come true and guiding them to build a business or a lifestyle that creates the freedom and financial security they have always wanted.

I have also learned to embrace the value of a plan. I always resisted planning, much like I avoided paying attention to my financials. It didn't feel fun, and there was always some better way to spend my time. I didn't get that planning would help me make more money more often, and with more profit. Now, I know where I am going and I know how to get there. I am prepared for the bumps in the road and the distractions. I no longer avoid my money, and I don't get that queasy feeling as frequently.

This book is all about helping you avoid the two massive mistakes that I made as a business owner: not having a plan in place for my business and ignoring my numbers. I promise to make this as fun, creative, and enticing as I can. If you are like me, you may be hearing the words *plan* and *numbers* and thinking about closing this book right now. Please don't. If you are committed to your own success, keep reading. We are just getting to the good stuff.

Your Complete Life Makeover

Do you feel like you could use a complete life or business makeover? I created a super fun mini art workshop to help you start dreaming about what that would look like to create. You can download this free workshop at

http://www.mindfulpatterns.com/life-makeover.

Chapter 3

Why Creative Entrepreneurs Struggle with Money

Did you recognize yourself in my money story in Chapter 2? Since I sold my business in Texas and moved to California, I have invested significant time and money in understanding who I am as a business owner and what I need to do differently to build a profitable business. Before I could begin to build a new business, I had to make peace with my relationship with money.

I have been able to take what I learned from my mentors and coaches and build a solid foundation for a business that I love. I leveraged everything I have learned about being a successful business owner to help my clients achieve the financial success they always dreamed of. I have helped them avoid some of the massive mistakes that I made the first time around. As I reflected on the past few years and all the clients I have worked with, I realized each of them shared a few key characteristics.

In this chapter, I will share some of the challenges of being a creative entrepreneur as well as some of the gifts. I will ask you some powerful questions, and I ask that you take the time to answer them. These questions will help you determine where you are stuck or overwhelmed in your current business. Once you identify where you are, you can see what your next best steps are for moving forward.

Remember those scary statistics that I shared in the introduction about women entrepreneurs? My goal is to get you out of that 94 percent of women business owners and into the 6 percent who are making six and even seven figures in their businesses! To do that, you need to understand why being a creative entrepreneur creates some additional challenges but also why it means you have some unique gifts that you can use to your advantage.

The Giant Billboard

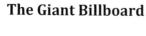

Let's do a quick Artsignment™ before we go any further. Part of your business success will come from creating a crystal-clear vision of what you want. We will work on that clarity throughout this book, but for right now I want to encourage you to have some fun. Take out your journal or some blank paper and complete the following sentences:

- This evening, I painted a giant billboard with my message to the world about my business. It said_____
- When I stepped back and looked at it, my first thought was _____
- Then I looked again and was surprised to see _____
- When I squinted my eyes, I suddenly saw _____
- When I spun round and round, I suddenly saw _____
- When I sat in my soul, I saw _____
- When I was perfectly still, I saw _____
- My message on this billboard looked like _____
- My message tasted like _____
- My message smelled like _____
- My message sounded like _____
- My message felt like _____
- My heart swelled with an invitation to share _____
- I finally knew it was time for my business to _____
- And I knew my very first step was to _____

There are no right or wrong answers to this assignment. Allow your business to start to show its playful side, its spiritual side, or whatever else it wants to express to you. Write as much as you want or as little as you want. Read back over what you wrote. What surprised you? What made you smile? What is one thing you could do today to nurture this vision of your business?

5 Biggest Challenges Creative Women Entrepreneurs Face that Keep Them Stuck at a 5-figure Income

1. Suffering from Bright, Shiny Idea Syndrome

Creative entrepreneurs tend to be full of fabulous ideas that are constantly flowing through their minds and often interrupt the current focus of their business day. This flow of ideas is so natural to them that they fail to see how much disruption it is causing or how it is impacting their bottom line.

The challenge lies in the inability of creative entrepreneurs to monetize these amazing ideas, not in the flow of ideas themselves. As you will see in the next section, these ideas are also a tremendous gift. Let me share a quick story with you about one of my clients. (Please note that while the stories I will share with you about my clients are all true case studies, I have changed their names to protect their privacy.)

Sarah came to me early this year wanting to start her own business as a coach or practitioner helping women deal with the stress of daily life. She is a bright, talented woman with several different degrees and training in a variety of areas. Some of the different tools she uses in her work with women are intuitive painting, yoga therapy, journaling, and traditional coaching methods.

Sarah had no idea how to take all of these different practices and methodologies, all of which she loves, and combine them into a coherent business that would attract her ideal client. She didn't even know who would want to work with her or what she would be helping them with. And she certainly didn't know how to charge for her services or how to advertise them.

Over the course of the year, I have watched Sarah be pulled by one idea after another. We would put a plan into place for one idea, and by our next coaching session, she would be off chasing another idea that sounded more fun. It has been a roller-coaster journey, by her own admission, to finally settle on one idea that Sarah felt confident to offer to others and to charge money for. Having too many ideas is just one of Sarah's challenges as a creative entrepreneur and first-time business owner.

After exploring different avenues and trying a few different things, Sarah did finally settle on coaching as the primary tool she wanted to use to help her ideal clients. She went out and found several people who were willing to do some sample coaching sessions with her. This helped her clarify if coaching was really something she wanted to do, plus it boosted her confidence to see how much she was able to help women solve their problems. She received invaluable feedback from her coaching sessions about what she did well, plus she got clarity about the specific problems she is best at serving. Now she is ready to launch a marketing campaign to get paying clients!

2. Overwhelming Fear of Marketing and Sales

Creative entrepreneurs are brilliant and talented at whatever they put their minds to. They are passionate about the work they do in the world, and they are called to serve the world on a larger scale. They know they need to get better at marketing and sales, yet they are terrified, overwhelmed, and confused.

Often they are confused by the technology and the modern ways business owners promote their businesses, such as websites, blogging, social media, online advertising, webinars, etc. Many creative entrepreneurs believe that if they just do a great job, work harder, and rely on word of mouth, they will be able to grow a profitable business. Nothing is further from the truth.

Creative entrepreneurs need to understand the relationship between marketing and sales. They need to learn how to price and package their services, and they need to gain confidence in their ability to sell themselves.

Let me tell you about my client Julie who has been a graphic designer for fifteen years. She is incredibly talented and has a steady stream of clients flowing in most of the time. She really wants to increase her income to the six-figure mark. When we started working together, she was stuck in three specific places in her business: (1) she was terrified of networking, so she wasn't meeting new people; (2) she knew she needed to update her website but was feeling creatively burnt out; and (3) she didn't have a plan in place for growing her business.

Her inability to finish her website was causing her to feel overwhelmed, anxious, and embarrassed. She didn't want to meet new people or send potential clients to her old website, so she stopped marketing. You can imagine what happened to her business with no marketing in place. She was suffering from some serious inconsistencies in her income and was stuck on the money roller coaster of feast or famine.

With some coaching, she was able to complete her website and fall in love with her business again. Once she got into action, we also created some fun marketing ideas for her business, and new clients started flowing in. We were able to increase the amount of business she was getting from her current clients, and she has a plan in place to make sure she is consistently marketing her business, even when she already has a steady flow of clients. She even attended a couple networking groups, and we were able to create a thirty-second commercial that was humorous, put her at ease, and still allowed her to feel good about her work as a designer.

Are you feeling stuck like Julie? What is holding you back in your business? Try the mindfulness tip below when you are feeling stuck, overwhelmed, or afraid.

Mindfulness Tip

When you find yourself feeling overwhelmed, fearful, or confused about some aspect of your business, take a time-out. Walk away from your desk—maybe go outside or find a quiet place in your home or office to sit down. Close your eyes. Center yourself by taking a few deep breaths. Feel your feet firmly connected to the earth. Stay present and focused on your breath. Imagine there is energy flowing from the earth's core up through the bottom of your feet, through your body, and out the top of your head, connecting you to the skies above. This energy flows in both directions, connecting you to earth and spirit and your own inner wisdom. Take a deep breath, hold it briefly, and release it slowly. Now ask yourself, "What is one action I can take to _____?" Fill in the blank with whatever you would like guidance about. Listen for the answer, and trust what comes. Slowly return to your breathing. When you feel complete, open your eyes. Return to your desk and take the inspired action you just received!

3. Marketing Only When New Business Is Needed

What I have seen over and over with my creative clients is that their marketing is inconsistent at best, even when they are clear about what they want to attract. When they have a full slate of clients and work to do, they stop marketing. Yikes! This is one of the biggest challenges most business owners face. **When you stop marketing, you create huge income gaps in your business.**

Creative entrepreneurs are passionate about the work they do and can easily get caught up in the joys and stresses of their day-to-day activities. They allow marketing activities to repeatedly fall to the bottom of their to-do list. When we looked at Julie's income over the past year, we could see why she had big gaps in her income. She would have so much work flowing in, she would stop networking or doing any marketing to attract new clients. Then, she would finish her current workload and suddenly find herself without any new work coming in for months at a time.

Idea Box: Take a look at your income flow over the past twelve months. Are there significant highs and lows? Where are the gaps? Can you remember what was happening in the month or two prior to the lows? This awareness of the financial flow of your business will help you see where the gaps are and why you need to be marketing consistently, even when your business is doing well.

4. Having No Marketing Plan at All

Julie's biggest challenge as a creative entrepreneur is that she doesn't like marketing or sales and has avoided having a plan that would require her to market herself.

I have seen this over and over again with my creative clients! To be completely honest, I have suffered from this myself. I do a lot of marketing, but I tend to err on the side of chasing the next big idea rather than having a consistent plan in place. Once I figured out that by just doing some advanced planning I could easily attract more clients, even when I'm not working, I started to get excited about planning.

Another challenge that creative entrepreneurs experience related to planning is that planning is boring. Planning is often perceived as a left-brained, linear activity requiring information about facts, figures, projections, and way too many details. All of this can be extremely intimidating to right-brained, visual creatives, including me. That's why it has become my passion and mission to create a visual marketing plan for creative entrepreneurs that makes planning for your business fun, flexible, and profitable. You will learn more about visual marketing plans in Chapter 10 when I share my unique Color Wheel Marketing Plan™ template.

To go back to the example of Julie, the graphic designer, we have been able to craft a marketing plan for her that is fun, doesn't take too much time, and is targeted specifically to the types of clients Julie most loves to work with. As she has steadily made progress this year with her business and her planning, she has created some great momentum in her business. Having a plan in place has not only increased her income but has also taken away some of the fear and those overwhelming feelings she had about marketing when we started.

 ## Capturing Your Business in a Collage

Creating what you want in your business happens on the practical, tangible levels. It also happens on the spiritual and emotional levels. When the personal and the practical are aligned, it's easier to manifest what you want in reality through a combination of taking action and being open to receiving. I invite you to create a collage that includes images that symbolize what you want to create.

Creative entrepreneurs are visual learners, so let's use that strength to build your business. Collage is an ideal format because you will be working with images. You can use a page in your journal, a large sheet of paper, or a small poster board. Grab a stack of magazines—the more variety the better. Select images that appeal to you or which seem to be meaningful, even if you can't exactly articulate what the meaning is. Fill the page with images only, no words.

When the collage is finished, spend a few moments journaling about what you notice. What feels powerful? What feels possible?

5. Being Numb to the Numbers

The biggest mistake that creative entrepreneurs make is that they are numb to their numbers. What do I mean by that? I mean that most creative entrepreneurs ignore, avoid, and fail to pay attention to the financial side of their business. As you saw in Chapter 2, this was one of the biggest challenges I personally experienced with my first business.

In Chapter 4 of this book, I will share more about why this is the biggest mistake creative entrepreneurs make and how to learn to love your numbers!

One of the lessons I learned in the past year is that I am good with numbers. I had the mistaken belief that because I wasn't good at math like algebra and geometry, then I also wasn't good at money. The truth is, money math is based on simple addition and subtraction that most of us learned in elementary school. Yet, here's what my clients often say about money:

- I don't understand it.
- It's too hard.
- Numbers scare me.
- I'm not good with numbers.
- I have no idea how much money I'm making.
- I don't know what numbers to pay attention to.
- What's a budget?

Creative entrepreneurs must learn to love their numbers if they want to build six-figure businesses. That doesn't mean you have to understand complicated systems; that's what bookkeepers and accountants are for. However, you do have to know the answers to these three simple questions:

- How much money do I want to make?
- How much am I currently making?
- How much am I spending?

I find that creative entrepreneurs struggle to answer even these simple questions about their businesses because they are numb to their numbers.

 Journaling Prompt

Take out your journal and answer the following questions:

- What would loving your numbers change for you?
- How would you act differently if you loved your numbers?
- What would you change in your business if you loved your numbers?

Creative Entrepreneurs Can Use Their Biggest Gifts to Break Through Their Money Plateau

I don't want to paint the picture that all creative entrepreneurs struggle or that they are incapable of building a profitable business. There are many examples of very successful creative entrepreneurs: artists, designers, authors, speakers, coaches, and others who are making six and seven figures in their businesses.

What do they know that most creative entrepreneurs don't?

1. They know how to use their gifts to their best advantage.

2. They know how to monetize their ideas.

3. They know how to ask for help.

Let's look at each of these in more detail.

1. Creative entrepreneurs never lack ideas about what to create next.

Yes, I know I said that too many ideas can be a challenge. Successful creative entrepreneurs value the flow of ideas, but they know how to manage the flow and focus on one at a time. They are often visionaries in their industry who see their gifts as a way to serve multitudes of people. Is that you? Do you know you have incredible gifts to share and are tired of being the best-kept secret in your industry?

When I was publishing a magazine every month, I had a built-in structure that allowed me to be creative yet still get things done. That magazine had hard deadlines that created a sense of urgency. I knew I had to get the files to the printer at a set date and time every month if I wanted to be able to distribute the magazines by the first of each month. My advertisers paid me good money in good faith that I would get their business out to my thousands of readers. This system worked well for me, and not once in eight years of printing the magazine did I ever miss a print deadline. In between those deadlines, I had the freedom to chase all kinds of bright, shiny ideas for selling more ads, appealing to new advertisers, or creating fun events to attract more readers.

Now that I'm working as a business coach, my income isn't tied to anyone else but me. There is no built-in structure, no hard deadline to get things done when it comes to finding new clients. I find that this is a challenge for me and for the creative entrepreneurs I work with. I can honestly say that after all those years of hard deadlines and the stress of getting the final proofs of the magazine to the printer, I was so relieved to not have those commitments. Now I write a blog post when I have an idea, schedule a webinar when I want, take an afternoon off if I feel like it.

I like my workdays to have a bit more flow and flexibility. I don't miss the rigid deadlines of the publishing industry.

But I also know that without some systems in place for monetizing and implementing all my ideas, I cannot build a profitable business. So I look for ways to create a structure that works for me but doesn't feel like a prison. Does that sound familiar?

Let me share another example with you. Mary is an entrepreneur who is married and has three teenaged boys. She was completely overwhelmed by all the to-dos on her list and the perceived pressure to get work done every day. Rather than supporting her to be productive, deadlines made her panic and shut down. She was such a perfectionist that she found herself deciding not to get anything done at all rather than do what she felt was a less-than-perfect job. She wanted the freedom to get up each morning and work on what felt the most fun and productive in the moment. She was afraid that if she relied on just her intuition to guide her in this process, nothing would get done! She didn't trust herself to work this way.

What we discovered in working together is that creative entrepreneurs need a combination of structure and freedom. I didn't want to believe it at first, but what I have learned in my fifteen years as an entrepreneur is that **systems will liberate you**! We have to work diligently and creatively to discover which systems are most effective and still allow us the freedom to go with our natural creative flow.

Create an Idea Box:

Here's a suggestion for one simple system to put into place that allows your creative ideas to flow unrestricted while preventing each new idea from taking over your life.

Keep a special notebook, binder, folder, file on your computer, or even a box that is just for your ideas. Every time you get a new idea, write it down somewhere—just be sure to collect all your ideas in one place. If you are a visual artist or designer, keep a visual record through photography, sketches, or magazine images that you add to your idea file. Say thank you to each idea and set it aside for later. In her book *The Creative Habit*, Twyla Tharp suggests creating a box to collect all the ideas for a particular project. She writes:

> The box makes me feel organized, that I have my act together even when I don't know where I'm going yet. It also represents a commitment. The simple act of writing a project name on the box means I've started work. ... Most important, though, the box means I never have to worry about forgetting. One of the biggest fears for a creative person is that some brilliant idea will get lost because you didn't write it down and put it in a safe

place. I don't worry about that because I know where to find it. It's in the box.

What successful creative entrepreneurs understand is that all ideas may have value at some point, but we can only focus on creating and monetizing them one at a time. By documenting the ideas, we can hold onto them and honor them without allowing them to distract us from the current project. A creative combination of flow and focus is necessary to sustain both creative genius and success.

In Mary's case, deadlines needed to be set far enough in the future that she could allow herself the time and pleasure of working on a project when she was feeling her creative juices flowing. Long deadlines also allowed for the normal interruptions of her work by her family life with three busy teen boys. What systems would support your creative flow of ideas?

2. Successful creative entrepreneurs love to serve people, and they love to get paid for it!

The second trait successful creative entrepreneurs share is knowing how to monetize their gifts. They are in business to turn a profit. They don't give away their time and talents. They appreciate their own value and know that when they are making money and being paid well, they have the energy to serve even more people.

Learning to appreciate themselves can be a challenge for creative entrepreneurs, especially if they are new in business. Creative entrepreneurs definitely wear their hearts on their sleeves and can be very sensitive to judgment from others. They often mistakenly think that if they charge less for their products and services, they will attract more clients. The opposite is true. When an entrepreneur undercharges for her products and services, people wonder why her prices are so low and question the quality of the work.

Gloria is a vocal coach I worked with who did not have a clear understanding of how much value she was giving her clients and how little she was actually making per hour. She kept making deals and offering discounts without considering the financial impact. When we did the math, she realized she was making only about $25 an hour when she thought she was making $75 to $100 an hour. After we redid her pricing and packaged her services to ensure that she was actually bringing home $75 an hour, she was surprised how easy it was to convince people to pay. Suddenly she was averaging over $5,000 a month in her business, every month. This year she made more in her business than she had ever done in her previous ten years of coaching. Not one person balked at the new pricing, and she feels like she is serving her clients better than she ever has before.

Another client, Susan, is an interior designer who was struggling with cash flow and also with asking her clients for the money owed her. We made some shifts in how she gets paid, asking for a retainer up front. This helped smooth out some of the income gaps that come from being an interior designer—you can have long periods of work without getting paid as projects shift and change. Once she realized how easy it was to ask and that clients were fine with paying a retainer, she gained confidence in her ability to ask for money and to raise her rates.

 Journaling Prompt

What would you do differently in your business if you were no longer afraid?

3. Successful creative entrepreneurs ask for help.

I think the biggest challenge I have seen with the creative clients I work with is the belief that they can do it all themselves or that they cannot afford to hire help. There is a reason that starving artists are starving. It's not that they don't make money; it's because they don't pay attention to the details of running their business and forget to take care of things like paying bills or maybe even buying groceries. They are caught up in their passion for their work or stuck in the drudgery of the day-to-day running of their business and forget that they need to take a break, breathe, and tend to their business as if they were tending to a child or spouse.

Successful, profitable businesses always require a team effort. None of us excels at every aspect of building a business. Understanding what we are best at and finding support in areas that challenge us is one of the quickest ways to bust through that six-figure barrier.

I have been working with two women business owners who have worked together for twenty-five years. Let's call them Jane and Karen. They have built a profitable business, but they have lost their joy and passion. Their relationship with each other feels strained and awkward. As we began the discovery process that each of my clients goes through, I could easily see where several of their biggest challenges were. First, they are working so hard in their business that they have lost sight of where they are going. This is a classic entrepreneurial mistake. Basically, these two women have just created a job for themselves, and they are working so hard on a day-to-day basis that they don't have the focus or energy to create a plan for where they are going.

As you can imagine, not having a plan means they feel stuck. They are not doing any marketing, and their business is only marginally profitable rather than wildly successful. As I am writing this book, we are working together to help them rediscover their own passion by creating a new vision of what's possible. One of the very first tasks on their to-do list is to hire a manager to run more of the day-to-day operations of their business so that they will have the time and energy to create systems, processes, and a plan to grow their business to the next level.

I would invite you to consider what aspects of your business you are holding onto that aren't serving you. What could be outsourced to someone else who could do a better job than you?

Mindfulness Tips

Creating a mindfulness practice is a powerful tool for creating and sustaining balance. We creative entrepreneurs are a passionate lot and at times we need silence, solitude and the opportunity for deep reflection. Mindfulness can feed our creativity in beautiful and surprising ways. It can also save us from feeling like we are overwhelmed and spinning out of control.

A mindfulness practice can take many forms. Here are a few of my favorites that only require five minutes or less to implement:

- Stand up, take a deep breath, touch your toes, raise your hands high overhead, circle your shoulders and then just stand still, taking 3 or 4 more deep breaths.
- Sit quietly for 5 minutes and breathe deeply.

- Take a short walk outside, taking time to look at what is around you and appreciate what you see.
- Make a list of 5 things you have to be grateful for
- Write in your journal.

Discover Where You Are Stuck in Building Your Six-figure Business

I want to share a series of questions with you that I share with each of my clients. These questions form the foundation of what I call the "One-Page Business Plan." As you saw before, creative entrepreneurs tend to struggle with linear plans that include too many details. Yet, you still need to have a plan in place. A simple business plan serves as your road map for the year ahead. You don't need to know all the steps right now, but you do need to know your destination and what you are working toward.

What happens to creative entrepreneurs who don't have a plan in place? They often feel lost, overwhelmed, or stuck in their business. They lack clarity, which means they lack consistency. They end up chasing ideas, trying every new marketing tactic that comes along, or simply avoiding marketing all together, hoping that clients will show up.

The solution for creative entrepreneurs is to create a business plan that captures both the basics and the essence of their business in a meaningful and visual format. Creating a visual, one-page business plan should feel fun, exciting, and motivating. My clients tell me that going through this process with me leaves them feeling clearer about their business than ever before. They feel excited to get into action, and the feelings of chaos and of being overwhelmed disappear.

Remember that creative entrepreneurs don't think like other people, and that's a good thing. We tend to think in circles and see connections where others don't. Most of us became entrepreneurs because we want the freedom and flexibility to do the work we love, when we want to. We rarely have a clear separation between our lifestyle and our business. Creative entrepreneurs tend to take a holistic approach to business success.

Here are the initial questions that I ask my clients as we begin the process of designing a six-figure business that is a match for all of who they are and that supports the many roles they play: business owner, spouse/partner, parent, community volunteer, adventure seeker, athlete, yogi ... you get the picture!

I encourage you to take the time to answer all of these questions before you read any farther. You will find a copy of these questions in the downloadable companion workbook to this book here:

http://www.mindfulpatterns.com/artful-marketer-book

Preparing to Create Your Visual Business Plan

In a journal or a document on your computer, answer the following questions:

You:

- What do you love doing more than anything else?
- What are your core values? Take the assessment in the companion workbook to discover your Top 10 core values.
- What does an ideal day in your business/life look like?
- What do you do in your free time?
- What is your big WHY? (This is what keeps you working every day.)
- Why YOU? What is your unique brilliance? What are you best at?
- Who else is doing what you do? What do you love/admire about their work? How are you unique?

Your Clients:

- Who is your IDEAL client, and are there enough of them in the world to create a thriving business?
- What PROBLEMS do you solve for this client?
- Why are you the BEST person to solve these problems?
- What services/products do you offer to solve these problems?

Your Money:

- What is your BOLD money goal for the next two months, six months, twelve months?
- What is your desired MONTHLY income?
- How many SALES do you need to make to reach that income?
- How many PEOPLE do you need to talk to in order to get those sales?
- What is your COST of doing business?

Your Team:

- Who is on your support team?
  - Friends/Family/Spouse
  - Mentor/Coach
  - Hired Team (Finances and Accounting, Web/IT, Art/Media, Management, Admin, etc.)
  - Strategic Partners (other business owners who target the same specific audience that you do)

Now that you have the answers to these questions, let's get creative! What happens with most business plans is that they end up in a binder collecting dust on the shelf, stuffed in a file folder in a drawer, or lost in the computer. I recommend creating a colorful and visual version of your business plan that you can proudly display in your office.

Creating a visual business plan will remind you that you do have goals and a plan in place for taking action. This is especially helpful on those bleary-eyed mornings when your bank account is low, the coffee isn't helping, and you have no idea what to do. Turn to your plan, remember your big WHY, and ask yourself: *"What does my ideal client need today?"* Take one action that will help you connect meaningfully with your ideal clients and generate new leads for your business.

What is a mandala?

The word *mandala* (pronunciation *mon-dah-lah*) is from the Sanskrit language and loosely translated means "circle." Mandalas are circular designs symbolizing the notion that life is never ending. Mandalas appear in most spiritual traditions throughout the world. Mandalas are designed to represent integration, wholeness, and balance, both within ourselves and throughout the world. Longchenpa, a Tibetan Buddhist, describes the mandala as "an integrated structure organized around a unifying center."

You will see in the visual business plan how I have organized the information to flow from the center outwards. Your financial goal is at the center of the mandala. Many creative entrepreneurs may struggle internally with the idea of putting money at the center of their cosmos. You will learn more in Chapter 4 about making peace with money and even learning to love money. I ask you to trust me for now and to put your bold money goal at the center of your visual business plan.

Creating Your Visual Business Plan

For this variation of a visual business plan, I chose to have you create a mandala (see sidebar.) This structure represents the individual elements as well as the overall essence of your business plan. Most creative entrepreneurs are focused on creating a lifestyle, not just a job. Approaching your business from a holistic perspective allows you to showcase all the different aspects of your business and lifestyle.

If the mandala doesn't appeal to you, I encourage you to take your answers to the questions above and put them into any visual format that works for you; flow charts, mind maps, doodles, cartoons, and vision boards are other creative tools for visual planning that work well. Here is an image of a sample, one-page visual business plan. You will also find a full-color version as well as a blank template in the companion handbook. If you have not already downloaded your handbook, download it here http://www.mindfulpatterns.com/artful-marketer-book.

Sample Visual Business Plan

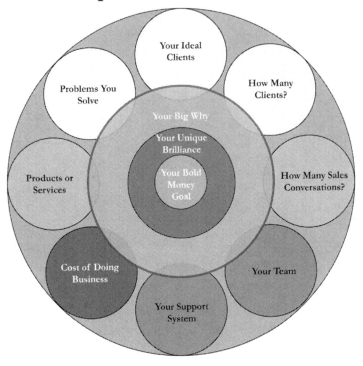

I encourage you to take the time to create your one-page business plan now before reading any farther in this book. Make your mandala business plan colorful and playful. Feel free to add images and words that you connect with or help you connect visually to what you want to create in your business. You could create this mandala by hand with crayons, markers or paint, and magazine cutouts. You could also create it digitally on your computer if that is your creative outlet. Whichever method you choose, just be sure to print it out or fill it out completely and hang it where you can see it!

Chapter 4

Learning to Love Money

Over the past few years, I have worked with dozens of women entrepreneurs who were struggling to build profitable businesses. They blamed their marketing, their fear of sales, and themselves for not knowing what to do. What I helped them see is that no business owner can create the freedom, flexibility, and financial independence that they crave until they understand their relationship with money. I have discovered that women entrepreneurs and especially creative women entrepreneurs struggle to stay connected to the financial aspects of their business. They will often say they didn't get into business to get rich but to be of service to others.

Until I figured this piece out for my own life and business, all the marketing in the world wasn't getting me the clients I needed to grow my business. Understanding my personal relationship with money helped me to heal the shame of not making money in my first business. It also helped me see how easy it is to stay focused on the financial details without feeling overwhelmed or confused.

Diving deep into my relationship with money, I learned how some of my core beliefs and family legacy around money were holding me back from creating the success I said that I wanted in my business. I discovered that I had some judgments and quite a few insecurities related to money because of the way I had been raised. Healing my relationship with money was the first step toward building a profitable business, and I can guarantee you that this one small step has generated tremendous growth—emotionally, spiritually, and financially.

How Healthy Is Your Relationship with Money?

Below is a short quiz that will give you some insight into your relationship with money. Read each statement and mark it with "True" or "False." You also have a printable version of this quiz in your companion handbook that you can download at

http://www.mindfulpatterns.com/artful-marketer-book.

1. I don't pay attention to where my money goes every month. I rarely even think about money.
2. I act as if I have plenty of money, but inside I'm always worried that I don't have
3. I don't deserve a lot of money when others have less than I do.

4. Things would get better if I had more money.
5. It's extravagant to spend money on myself.
6. I always have just enough money to live on.
7. I have plenty of money in savings for a rainy day.
8. I worry about money constantly.
9. Money isn't as important to me as being of service to others.
10. I know exactly how much money I make each month and how much my expenses are.
11. Making money is easy for me. I can always get money when I need it.
12. The more money I make, the more I spend.
13. I don't like to talk about how much money I have or make.
14. Those who don't have money are probably not trying hard enough.
15. Money would solve most of my problems.
16. I'm tense, and my stomach is in knots when I think about my finances.
17. I feel a little intimidated by people with lots of money.
18. I dread sitting down and paying my bills every month.
19. I buy things on credit cards that I know I can't pay for when the statement comes.
20. I get confused when making money decisions.
21. I prefer for someone else to make all the money decisions.
22. Spending money on myself makes me feel better.
23. I wish I didn't have to think about money or plan for the future.

Count up your responses to each of the twenty-three statements. If you answered "true" to five or more of the questions, it's time to look more deeply into your relationship with money. The more you are able to understand your attitudes, beliefs, and values around money, the more you will be able to feel in control of your own financial destiny and create financial freedom in your life.

Healing Your Relationship with Money Starts Here

In this section, I want to share with you some ideas on how to begin healing your relationship with money. I encourage you to download the companion workbook at http://www.mindfulpatterns.com/artful-marketer-book so that you can write your answers down in the spaces provided.

Your Family's Money Story

The first step to healing your relationship with money is to reflect on what you were taught about money or how you witnessed others close to you relating to money. I encourage you to get out your journal and a pen or download the companion workbook. Begin this process now!

Answer any of the following questions that resonate with you or are a match for your family relationships:

1. What did I learn about money from my grandparents?

2. What did I learn about money from my mother? Was it obvious or subtle?

3. What did I learn about money from my father? Was it obvious or subtle?

4. How did I perceive money as a child?

5. Did my family have a lot of money, not enough, or just enough money?

6. How did my family talk about other people who had money?

7. What type of work ethic did my parents have?

8. What do I believe to be true about money or wealth because of how I was raised?

Your Personal Relationship with Money

Are you starting to see how your relationship with money was influenced by the environment and attitudes of those you grew up with? Reflect on how you have treated money in the past. What are the connections between your family's money story and your personal connection to money? Look at your responses to the questions from the healthy money quiz. Can you see how you have either adopted your family's beliefs about money or have rejected them and chosen to do the opposite?

In order to help you be clear and honest about your relationship with money, take a minute to fill in the following blanks. There are no right or wrong answers to any of these questions. Be completely honest. No one will see your answers unless you choose to share them.

I have always treated money with _____.

I believe that people with lots of money are _____.

I say I want to make money, but the truth is _____.

If I could change one thing about my relationship with money, I would _____.

If I had lots of money, I would be _____.

When it comes to making money in my business, I'm going to _____.

 Envisioning a Healthier Connection to Money

Now that you are beginning to get a sense of what your relationship with money has been like in the past, you can begin to make changes. You can also begin to see what's possible for you and for your business when you learn to love money. Take a minute to create a new vision of your relationship with money. It's time to get out the markers and get creative. Let's create a word collage and have some fun with the positive and powerful possibilities that money holds for you.

Instructions on How to Create a Word Collage

1. Take a blank sheet of paper, the bigger the better. I love to use inexpensive kids' drawing pads that you can get at the dollar store, Walmart, or Target. Write the word MONEY in the center of paper and draw a circle around it.

2. Next, add any words that come to mind that are related to money. Some examples might be *abundance, wealth, riches, gold, treasure, gratitude, service, joy, happiness,* etc. Again, there are no right or wrong words; just write everything that comes to you. Feel free to use different colors and different sizes or styles of writing.

3. When you have written all the words that are at the top of your mind, read what you have written and add three more words. Continue this process until you are certain you have written down every word that you can think of related to MONEY.

Look at you word collage. What do you notice? How are you feeling in this moment? Looking at this beautiful money word collage that you have created, what is one action step that you can commit to taking in the next twenty-four hours to improve your relationship with money?

Why am I asking you to commit to taking one specific action in the next twenty-four hours? All the reading, writing, and drawing in the world will not help you build a profitable business unless it's combined with action. Taking one action step will create momentum. From that one step, you will know exactly what to do next. Perhaps you are feeling inspired right now and know what your next five steps need to be. Great! Write them down and commit to completing one at a time. The more we commit to our success, the more success will find us.

I am also asking you to take this specific action so that you can see how making even small changes in your relationship with money can have a BIG impact on your bottom line. I will tell you what I mean by this in the next section.

Chapter 5

Money Mistakes that Creative Entrepreneurs Make

I have discovered that creative entrepreneurs often make at least one of the following five common mistakes that stop them from building a profitable business. These mistakes stem from their beliefs about money, their family's money story, and their huge hearts. They also stem from fear of being judged by others. Below, you will find the five mistakes along with some specific examples of how these mistakes impacted the business success of creative entrepreneurs. You may find some of the information in this book to be repetitive, but there are a few key mindset shifts that are important to capture. Perhaps this version of the story will resonate with you.

Mistake #1 – Not charging what you are worth!

What I have seen over and over again with creative women entrepreneurs is that they undercharge for their services and products. They tend to pick numbers out of the air, basing their pricing on intuition or by comparing themselves to what others are doing. If you are new in business, I want you to pay close attention to this section. Don't let fear stop you from creating a profitable business.

There are many reasons entrepreneurs are afraid to charge what they're worth, but fear of rejection is number one on the list. Not charging what you're worth stems from the fear that people won't pay or you don't have enough experience. The truth is that people are most likely to pay for a product or service when the value is clearly communicated. People buy solutions and are willing to pay lots of money for them. Look at the weight-loss and cosmetic-surgery industries. They do a great job of convincing women that they have to pay billions of dollars a year to look younger, thinner, smarter, sexier. When you are wishy-washy in your offer or unclear about the results someone will receive from working with you, people won't trust you and they won't buy from you, no matter how much or how little you charge.

Let me share an example with you of a parenting coach who was afraid to charge more for her services. Maria lives in a big city with her husband and two school-aged kids. She loves the flexibility that her coaching business provides but knows she needs to increase her income. Her rent is going up, and her husband is a schoolteacher whose salary has been their sole financial support for several years. She is feeling a renewed sense of urgency about contributing to her family financially.

When we started working together, her goal was to be able to consistently bring in $3,000 per month to help cover her family expenses. Maria felt clueless about how to do this. What she had been trying wasn't working. She was afraid to raise her rates with her current clients, and she often struggled asking for the money from new clients, making that conversation feel awkward and uncomfortable.

Maria is a phenomenal coach who is solving real problems for families. Her big mindset shift came when she realized that she was focusing on selling the wrong things. Rather than focusing on results, she was trying to sell tools and her expertise. When Maria realized that what she was really selling was her commitment to helping her clients and her clear confidence in her ability to change their lives, she instantly felt better about raising her rates, and she learned how to state her new rates with confidence.

A powerful way to move through fear is to be reminded of the amazing work that you do in the world. You can read through testimonials you already have, or you can reach out and ask clients for feedback.

Ask three of your favorite clients what they have loved most about working with you and what specific results they have created because of their work with you.

Mistake #2 – Giving away your time and services for free!

Many creative entrepreneurs go one step farther than undercharging: they give away their products and services for free. Again, this stems from fear and lack of perceived value in their own ability to change lives. It also stems from two other problems: being too generous and not establishing strong boundaries in their practice.

Let me share the example of my client Nancy who is a massage therapist. Nancy loves what she does, and she knows she is good at it. She loves being of service to her clients and often keeps clients for many years. Her problem is that she never seems to make enough money or to attract enough new clients. Her schedule always seems full, and she can't understand what she's doing wrong.

When we sat down and looked at how Nancy was spending her time and what she was charging for her massages, we discovered that she consistently went over on her time but never charged the client extra money for time spent. Nancy did not create a system for staying on time with her clients, and she felt that if the client needed a little extra work here or there, she would just spend a few extra minutes. Plus, she spent time at the beginning and end of each session chatting with clients and checking in with them. She realized that while she was charging a client for a one-hour massage, she was often spending two hours with them. Yikes! You can see how that would impact her bottom line. She was basically giving her clients a whole hour of her time for free. Sometimes a client would offer to pay for the extra time, and she would refuse the money.

While I appreciate Nancy's love for her clients and willingness to take great care of them, her lack of focus on money and her failure to charge what she's worth or to respect boundaries cost her thousands of dollars a year.

Where in your business are you giving away your time, and how much is it costing you?

Mistake #3 – Afraid to be perceived as "salesy."

Creative entrepreneurs perceive themselves as artists, designers, nurturers, authors, coaches or whatever label they apply to themselves. They often see themselves as experts in their industry and have invested time and money perfecting their craft. However, they never perceive themselves as salespeople. In fact, creative entrepreneurs would often rather be broke than have to go door-to-door selling.

The hard truth is that if you are in business for yourself, then you are in the business of marketing and sales! No matter what type of work you do, you have to be able to promote yourself and speak with confidence about what you offer. This can be especially challenging for our introverted creative types who love their craft but struggle with talking about themselves. Book 2 in the Mindful Patterns series will address the topic of sales more directly, sharing how creative entrepreneurs can overcome their fear of sales. In this book, I will show you how effective marketing can generate leads that will clamor to buy from you!

Earlier in this section I told you about Maria, who was undercharging for her services and afraid to ask for more money. As we talked about marketing strategies and where Maria would most likely find and attract her ideal clients, she had a big A-ha! moment. She hates being sold to and finds most marketing language offensive and condescending. She was actively refusing to use language that would attract clients because it didn't feel good to her.

Many creative entrepreneurs struggle with the language of marketing just like Maria did. She did not want to be perceived as a used-car salesman with tricks and deals up her sleeve. The shift in mindset occurred when I helped Maria realize that marketing is all about getting people to notice you by showing them you understand the pain they are in and by educating them about how you can stop their pain. Like I said before, people buy solutions, and they buy results. When you are clear about your value and your ability to make a difference with the work you do, it's easy to convince people to buy from you, without feeling "salesy."

Reframing Your Perspective on Marketing.

Now that we have talked at length about why marketing is scary, let's make marketing fun again. In this short assignment, you will be using your creative writing skills to look at marketing through the lens of metaphor. In case you don't remember your high school or college English classes, a metaphor is a figure of speech in which a word or phrase that ordinarily designates one thing is used to designate another, thus making an implicit comparison. Some common metaphors include: heart of stone, time is money, or a blanket of snow.

Take out your journal and let's play with metaphor. It's time to reframe your perspective on marketing and remember that marketing can be fun, playful, meaningful and heart-centered. There is no right or wrong way to do this. You can use comparisons or create similes using like or as if that is easier. Just start writing and see what you discover. Here are a couple of examples that I created to help get you started.

- Marketing wears a big red nose to get attention.
- The glow of the marketing magic lit her up from the inside out.
- My marketing robot can do that for me.
- I use a rainbow of marketing tactics to grow my business.

Make MARKETING funny

Make MARKETING spiritual

Make MARKETING old-fashioned

Make MARKETING high-tech

Make MARKETING larger-than-life

Make MARKETING very small

Make MARKETING colorful

Make MARKETING YOU

There are no right or wrong answers. No one will judge your responses. Tap into your inner poet and allow metaphors to flow freely. Be as silly and far-fetched as you can.

Mistake #4 – Not taking responsibility for your finances.

What does it mean to take responsibility for your finances? It means that you pay regular, close attention to the cash that flows in and out of your business. You know how much debt you have, and you have a plan to pay it off. You have a budget, and you stick to it. My mentor, Kendall Summerhawk, would add that you have a weekly financial date with yourself and that you are tracking your income daily.

This is one that I have struggled with over the years. I ignored money until I had to face it. In college, I would put off paying bills, even if I had the money. I just didn't want to deal with it. It's sad to think about how much I paid out over the years in late fees because I was disorganized and didn't care about money.

Creative entrepreneurs care more about their work, the people in their lives, having fun, and serving others than they do about making money. In some cases, they think they aren't good with money and don't have a head for numbers. Your answers to the healthy money quiz might reflect some of these struggles.

In chapter 2, I shared how my husband and I were able to relocate to Santa Barbara, California, buy a house, and enjoy a flexible lifestyle that we had been dreaming of for years. The number one reason we were able to make this move happen is that we took 100 percent responsibility for our finances. We learned how to manage our debt, we focused on saving money, and we created a budget. We cut back our expenses and took money seriously. Not only did we make the move, we arrived with money in the bank and without creating any new debt. This was an incredible feeling of success that helped teach me that I am good with money when I try.

Where in your life are you continuing to ignore or avoid the truth of your financial situation?

I want to share another story about Julie, the graphic designer. Julie also struggles with paying attention to the financial details of her business and usually puts it all off until the end of the year. One of the interesting things I noticed about Julie was that she was not celebrating her financial success. In 2013, Julie made over $100,000 for the first time in her business. She acted like this was no big deal, and deep down she feared she wouldn't be able to do it again.

Julie had one client who had spent $40,000 on graphic design and printing in 2013. She ended up losing that client through no fault of her own, and she knew that she would not see that kind of income from another client in the coming year. Julie assumed that meant she wouldn't hit the six-figure mark again in 2014. When I started working with Julie, she was depressed, stuck, and overwhelmed. She'd had a few slow months that had her feeling very anxious about her business. After working together for six months, Julie is on track to bring in close to $90,000 in 2014, without that one big client.

One of the mindset shifts Julie needed to make was believing that she could consistently generate six figures in her business but she also needed to celebrate her wild success of the year before. Previous to 2013, Julie was averaging around $55,000 to $65,000 a year. It's hard to celebrate your success if you aren't paying attention to it. Julie is one of my many clients who are perfectionists. She is so hard on herself and always thinks she can be doing better. Part of our work together this year has been about paying regular attention to the money flowing into her business, expressing gratitude for her amazing clients, and celebrating the consistent progress she is making.

Are you failing to pay attention to how much money is flowing into your business on a regular basis? Start celebrating by tracking your income daily and expressing gratitude for every dollar flowing into your business.

Mistake #5 – You don't have a marketing plan in place.

Finally, Mistake #5 is what this book is all about. Creative entrepreneurs don't plan because they don't like marketing, they don't want to be confined by a schedule, or they are overwhelmed by all the different ways they can market their business so they either spread themselves too thin—trying a little of too many different things—or they throw their hands up in confusion and fail to do any marketing at all.

I will talk more about Mistake #5 throughout the book as well as how to create a marketing plan that is visual, meaningful, and profitable. But before we get to the marketing, I want to share two more sections on learning to love your money by taking responsibility for it. I also want to share more about the direct connection between your relationship with money and your mindset around marketing and sales.

Chapter 6

Best Practices for Learning to Love Money

In this section I'm going to share four best practices for learning to love your money. These are easy-to-implement tips that will help you avoid the mistakes most creative entrepreneurs make that I outlined in the last section. As with losing weight or starting an exercise regimen, taking care of your money needs to become a regular habit. These tips were inspired by Kendall Summerhawk.

In 2014 I became certified as a Sacred Money Archetype® coach. You can learn more about this process and take a free Sacred Money Archetype® Assessment here http://minetteriordan.com/money/. Learning your Sacred Money Archetypes® will help you troubleshoot the money blind spots that are likely creating an "invisible ceiling" over your income. This information will help you see the key areas where you may be giving away your power with money and will help you identify steps you can take to own your value—with confidence and clarity—so that you no longer make the common mistakes I outlined in the last chapter.

Tip #1 – Clear Your Money Clutter

If it feels unfinished, unresolved, messy, and complicated, or if it's something you've been avoiding, it's money clutter!

#1 Who Owes You Money

ACTION: Write down every company or person who owes you money and the amount they owe. Contact each of those companies or people and find out where your money is.

#2 Bills and Receipts Clutter

ACTION: Create one folder labeled "bills to be paid," then remove all your bills from countertops, piles, etc. and put them into the folder.

#3 Schedule Your Payments

ACTION: Create a schedule (weekly is best) for paying bills and mark the day and time in your calendar. Keep this appointment as your "money date" each week.

#4 Using Gift Cards

ACTION: Gather up all your unused gift cards and gift certificates, cash them in, use them, or spend them in the next seven days.

#5 Gathering Loose Money

ACTION: Gather up all your loose change and then exchange it for bigger bills and spend it in the next seven days. You can spend it on yourself, or you can put it toward debt.

#6 Lighten Your Wallet

ACTION: Take out your wallet and clear out the clutter. If your wallet is torn, worn, or shabby, replace it with one that is new and that makes you happy.

Tip #2 – Start Tracking Your Income

In your companion workbook you will find a sample tracking sheet that you can use to track your income on a daily basis. Yes, I did say *daily*. Trust me, I know this sounds extreme! But also trust me when I say that tracking your income is one of the quickest ways to get it flowing in faster. Why? Because what we focus on grows!

When you start tracking your income daily, it can be painful to see day after day with a zero on it. Those zeroes can motivate you to take action and do a better job of promoting yourself.

Seeing numbers flowing in day after day reminds you to be thankful for every penny! I have even added in the pennies I find in parking lots and refund checks from an insurance overpayment. Tracking your income is about paying attention to all the abundance that is coming your way! I would also include tax refunds or other payments that don't come specifically from clients. Money is money is money. Pay attention to it.

Tip #3 – Create a Gratitude Ritual

Once you start tracking your money, I also want you to create a gratitude ritual for every client payment that comes in. Again, this is a way of taking responsibility for your finances and paying attention to the details. One of the things I asked Julie to do was to say "thank you" to every payment that came in and to do a happy dance in her living room or office.

You might put a gold star on your calendar, kiss the check, do a happy dance, or start a gratitude spreadsheet. Simply take a few moments to say "thank you." It doesn't matter *how* you acknowledge the money flowing in; it matters that you do. Expressing gratitude will stop you from feeling overwhelmed or stuck. It will remind you that you are great at what you do and that people are already happily paying you for your products and services.

Idea Box: Create a gratitude purse—this could mean decorating a small bag or a used wallet or purse. Then each time you are aware of something you are grateful for, write it on a slip of paper and put it in the purse. This "spare change" symbolizes the changes you are making in your life and your new prosperity awareness.

"Gratitude is the best way I know to suddenly 'win the mental lottery,' so to speak. Nothing can make you feel better, richer, and more alive than being constantly, consistently aware of all of your blessings." – Marney Madrikakis

Tip #4 – Set a Financial Date with Yourself

This is a hard one for me: I don't like looking at my numbers, especially if there is no money flowing in. But I have learned that the more I notice what is happening—good or bad—the more motivated I am to take action and make positive changes.

I encourage you to set a financial date with yourself at least twice a month. Many people say you should do it weekly, but I know that is a stretch for creative entrepreneurs. This date does not need to be longer than fifteen minutes, but it does need to be scheduled on your calendar so that you commit to the time.

During this date, pay attention to what has flowed in as well as what has flowed out and what you owe. Are you trying to pay down debt? This is a great time to see if you have extra money to add to your payment. Are you trying to save for something big, such as a new business coach or a new car? Look at your finances and find a few extra dollars to add to your savings plan.

Taking these small actions can have a big financial impact on your business!

What Is the Connection Between Money, Marketing, and Sales?

When I first considered writing this book, my intention was to focus on just the marketing aspect and teach people how to create an effective marketing plan for their creative business. As I began to reflect on the work I have been doing with my clients and what I personally have learned this year, I realized that there was more to the story.

Yes, creative entrepreneurs struggle with marketing and sales, but they also struggle with their mindset around money. I knew I would not be setting readers of this book up for success if I didn't address their relationship with money.

Without a healthy respect for money and a clear understanding of the financial situation of your business, no marketing or sales training in the world will help you build a profitable business. A great marketing plan and some new sales training might help you make more money, but it won't help you hold onto the money you are making or make a profit.

Remember Nancy, the massage therapist? She had great clients, and she was serving them well, but she wasn't valuing her time. The money flowing in wasn't enough to cover her time and expenses.

Without a proper understanding of your cost of doing business, you may be undercharging for your services or constantly working harder rather than smarter. If you are someone who just guesses at what to charge or trusts your intuition on pricing, you may be struggling to create financial freedom. Don't get me wrong—I believe in the power of intuition to guide us in our business, but I have learned the hard way that I have to know my numbers intimately. Trusting intuition is used too often as an excuse for ignoring or avoiding our finances.

What Creative Entrepreneurs Have to Learn about Money

Creative entrepreneurs have to learn three things about money if they are going to build a six- or seven-figure business.

1. They have to know how much it costs to do business and how much they want to make.
   Go back to your one page business plan. What is your bold money goal for the coming year? Do you have a plan to get you there? This is the place to start. If you are not sure about how to get started, make a list of all your expenses on a monthly basis. Compare that to how much you are making every month. The difference between those two numbers, what you are spending and what you are making, is your profit. How much more profit would you like to generate in your business?

2. They have to understand that marketing is simply lead generation. Marketing is not scary; it's what helps people identify with a business so that they want to hire them.

3. They have to know how to price and package their services.

   The biggest money mistake I see creative entrepreneurs make is that they don't charge enough for their products and services. If you value yourself and what you offer by charging what you are worth, and if you market yourself in a way that shows others how you can help them, the sales will be easy.

By now, you should have a better understanding of your relationship with money. You have some practical tips for learning to love money, and you know that you must accept 100 percent responsibility for your finances if you want to see them grow. Learning to love money is a process, especially if this information is new to you and you have spent most of your life ignoring or avoiding money like most creative entrepreneurs do. Be gentle with yourself. Start putting some of the best practices in place.

If you are feeling overwhelmed, pick one practice to begin with. I would start with tracking your income. Start to notice the patterns in your business and feel grateful for the abundance flowing in. I encourage you to work on your relationship with money just like you would work to improve any relationship in your life. Take care of it, nurture it, and learn to love it.

Chapter 7

The Difference between Marketing and Sales

Working with business owners and salespeople over the past ten years, I've come to realize that few people understand the difference between marketing and sales. We all talk about needing to increase sales and revenue, but few of us realize that in order to do that, we have to get better at our marketing in order to attract more of the clients who are interested in buying from us. We are spending too much time, money, and effort trying to sell to everyone instead of focusing on the people who are looking for a solution to a certain problem, whether they know it or.

Callan Rush, one of my favorite marketing experts and educators, talks about what she calls education-based marketing. She says that we have to give value first and then position our purpose. She convincingly argues that only 3 percent of our specific audience is actively shopping at any given moment for a solution and that all our competitors are targeting that same 3 percent of people. If we take an education-based approach to marketing, we can successfully target an additional 67 percent of our specific audience. 30 percent of people are an absolute no, for whatever reason. Don't waste effort marketing to this group. You do, however, want to focus time, money, and effort marketing to the 67 percent in the middle.

For me, marketing is everything I do to attract and persuade potential clients to use my services. That's all it is. What can I do to attract people to me? Offer what Rush calls education-based marketing, which is marketing that solves problems for people.

For example, I owned a magazine that is all about kids and families. A health care company that offers nursing assistance to the elderly would not be a client for me, so why would I spend time and money marketing to ALL health care companies in Dallas when I could help only the ones who serve children?

What we want to develop is an attraction-based marketing plan versus what I sometimes call push-based marketing—where I feel like I'm pushing myself onto people, desperately trying to sell. This feels like a stereotypical used-car salesman approach, and most creative entrepreneurs are terrified that they will be perceived in this way.

Creative entrepreneurs want people lining up and saying, "Hey, you! Yes, you! I want to do business with you." You can make this happen with the right type of marketing, but it often requires a dramatic shift in your mindset and approach to marketing. The key is to define exactly what your potential clients need from you and what problems you can solve for them. You combine that with what your great at, and you find your "sweet spot." Most businesses owners are trying to convince **everyone** that they are the best by focusing on themselves. Creative business owners spend too much time and energy trying to prove their expertise instead of focusing on the results they are creating for others. Great salespeople know that it's never about them. It's always about what the client wants and needs.

Have you heard the adage that people love to buy, but hate to be sold? Is that true for you? You like to purchase things, but you don't like pushy salespeople trying to convince you to buy, right? I traveled quite a bit for business last year, and I noticed that they are trying to increase sales in airports. I would stop at a kiosk or shop to buy some mints or a bottle of water. The cashier would say, "Sure you don't need some nuts to go with that?" It made me giggle internally. They are just doing their job, and most of them weren't being pushy, but they were offering something I wasn't looking for and trying to persuade me to spend more money. That is not attraction-based marketing.

The trick to marketing success is to make sure there are enough people coming toward you that want to work with you. Once you realize that marketing is about attraction and about being of service and cultivating relationships, you can begin to construct a plan that makes marketing fun. In my experience, creative entrepreneurs want to be of service, want to love their clients, and want to make money, but they also want to avoid sales and marketing. If you can shift your mindset to focus on marketing as another avenue of service that solves problems for people, it will make attraction-based marketing easy as well as meaningful!

Now that I have clarified how I define marketing, let me clearly identify the difference between marketing and sales. Marketing is everything I do to attract and persuade people to move toward using my service. In four short words: marketing is lead generation. Sales is what I do to ensure that they sign the dotted line and pay their bill. Sales is taking them from being a window-shopper or blog-hopper to being a paying client.

If marketing is simply making sure the right people are attracted to your business, here are a couple questions you must be able to answer:

- Are you clear about who your specific audience is? You cannot market to everyone! We will discuss this at length in chapter 10.

- What tools or marketing tactics are you currently using? Are you sure you are getting your name in front of the right clients, the ones who already want what you are selling?
- Are you spending too much time, money, and effort trying to sell to everyone instead of selling to the people who want to buy what you have to sell? Remember our 67 percent? That is who we want to attract.

Chapter 8

Twelve Marketing Mistakes Creative Entrepreneurs Make

If you are going to effectively grow your business, then there are twelve marketing mistakes you should be aware of. You will not grow your business beyond your current revenue level if you don't effectively learn how to market yourself and the services you offer.

Marketing is a mindset that you have to cultivate on a daily basis.

Let me share the story of Tom and his brother with you in order to illustrate where we are going in this chapter. Tom wrote, "My brother and I decided one of the ways we would make money for ourselves was to create a lawn-cutting business. Being the astute and smart person that I was, I decided I would figure out how to build the best lawn-care business I could. I made sure I had a really good lawn mower. I actually turned the lawn mower over and made sure I had the sharpest blades. I knew if I created a pattern for doing people's lawns and made that lawn look great, I'd have a great business and I could make myself some money.

My younger brother, Stan, on the other hand, borrowed whatever lawn mowers he could find. He would often borrow lawn mowers from the people whose lawn he mowed. Within about two weeks, Stan was cutting lawns for six people around the city. While I was still trying to figure out how to sharpen my blade, my brother was raking in the money. What I realized very quickly and what I learned from my brother, which bothered me because he was my younger brother, was that he had all this money coming in and he'd created this really cool business. While he was making money, I was focused on building my lawn-care business. He was focused on marketing his lawn care services.

While I was cleaning my lawn mower, he was knocking on people's doors, saying, 'We've got this cool business.' He had so much business he was hiring people in his class to help him. That's the difference. If you don't get that, eventually you'll end up like I did, sitting by the side of the road with no business because I didn't know how to market myself."

Tom learned several valuable lessons that summer that illustrate the massive mistakes that creative entrepreneurs make. The key difference between Tom and his brother was mindset. By the end of this chapter, I would love to see you creating a whole new mindset about yourself as a marketer.

Marketing Mistake #1 – Not seeing yourself as a marketer.

The fundamental mistake creative entrepreneurs make is that they don't see themselves in the business of marketing their service or product. They just see themselves as a business owner or service provider, whatever the job is that they do. The truth is that you are a marketer. If you don't see yourself as a marketer, you'll never grow your business.

I would imagine that you started your business because you believe you have the credentials, gifts, talents, and passion for helping people. I know that's why I'm in business—to be of service to others. But being a coach, artist, therapist, writer, graphic designer, or whatever the work is that you do as a creative entrepreneur is not the business you're in. You are in the business of marketing. Without marketing, you have no business.

Mistake #2 – Thinking that people care about you and your business.

I hate to tell you this, but nobody cares about your business. Doesn't that make you feel good? Nobody cares about your business, your passion, or your credentials. One of the assumptions we creative entrepreneurs make is that people care about what we do. What I've discovered in my own businesses is this: people don't care about the *how*, and they don't care about my tools, training, or processes. What people care about is themselves. They care about their nagging pains, their problems, and their predicaments, what I will fondly refer to throughout this book as the Three Ps.

Let me ask you why you picked up this book. If can guess, it's because you are not currently attracting as many clients or making as much money as you'd like. Am I right? Or perhaps you were attracted to the creative elements of the book because you perceive yourself as a creative entrepreneur?

Your specific audience will only bother to think about you or what you can offer them if somehow you touch them where their pain is or where their problems are. The mistake many creative entrepreneurs make is thinking people will automatically care about what we're offering in the world. People are looking for a solution to their problems. Your job as a marketer is to show them why your solution is the best one.

Mistake # 3 – Believing that because you have a business, you will get business.

I see this so often with clients of mine. They believe in the "field of dreams" model of business. You remember *Field of Dreams*, the movie? "If you build it, they will come." The reality is people don't come just because you build it. When I owned the publishing company, I would see this happen time after time. New business owners would spend tens of thousands of dollars to promote a grand opening, and no one would show up. They would send out thousands of mailers, put up balloons and banners, send out press releases, and pray that people would show up. Then they would realize that they had spent all their marketing dollars for an entire year on one event that didn't drive people to their store, and they didn't understand why. Grand openings are all about "Look at me! Look at what I built!" They are not focused on building relationships or solving problems for a specific group of people.

Mistake #4 – Not understanding what makes you unique.

You should know what makes you different, what makes your business special, and you should tell everybody. Most small companies cannot afford large branding campaigns. Don't try to be Coca-Cola! People make the mistake of thinking: "If I just get my name out there enough, all of a sudden people will buy my service or product." It is a mistake to think that because you get your name out there to hundreds or even thousands of people they will buy your service or product. Getting your name out there is important, but you have to do it in a way that is attractive, educational, and puts you in front of the right people, not all people.

There is also a tendency to try to make our marketing look like what we think "Marketing" should be. Perhaps you are comparing yourself to other experts in your industry, or perhaps you believe that marketing is advertising. Advertising is a tactic and can be used effectively, but it has to be done right. Stop trying to look, talk, and act like anyone else. Attraction-based marketing requires you to be original and unique. You don't have to spend thousands of dollars creating a brand to do this. Your unique brand will evolve over time.

I would encourage you stop worrying about what others in your industry are doing and start focusing on two things: What makes you unique? What makes you most attractive to your perfect clients?

Remember, marketing is about being attractive, not pushing your message out into the world. It's about speaking directly to the people who already want what you have to offer so that they can self-select.

Marketing Mistake #5 – Fear of choosing a particular niche or specific audience to target in your marketing.

You will hear me harp on this topic over and over again throughout this book. If you learn one thing, it's that I want you to understand that you must narrow the focus of your business to one particular type of person. Your goal as a business owner is to market to one person instead of to everyone. When you try to market to everyone, you tend to reach no one. It makes it impossible for people to self-select because they don't recognize themselves or their problems in your marketing. It also makes it very difficult for others to send you referrals because your marketing is so vague they don't know who to send your way.

Creative entrepreneurs often fear that if they narrow their marketing to target one type of person, they will miss out on business or not attract enough business. Strangely, the reverse is true. The more you focus on solving problems for a particular niche, the more you become an effective and valuable commodity to that niche. They see you as an expert because they know you understand their problem, pain, and predicament. It's important that you understand why you must find a target audience or a group of people you understand. It doesn't mean you have to have their same problems; it just means you understand their Three Ps. Secondly, it does not mean you should have only one niche. It means that when you market to people, you market to one niche at a time with a focused, targeted approach instead of trying to be everything to everybody.

Secret tip: Have you noticed that throughout this book I have focused on creative entrepreneurs? I could have focused on women entrepreneurs, small business owners, graphic designers, etc. I'm very clear about who my specific audience is and what problems are at the top of your mind. What I am teaching in this book would work for any business owner, but I don't want to work with all business owners. I want to work with smart, creative women entrepreneurs who struggle with marketing themselves.

Marketing Mistake #6 – Failure to create and implement a marketing plan.

I see this happen over and over again with creative entrepreneurs. When creative entrepreneurs fail to have a marketing plan, marketing happens haphazardly at best. Why do creative entrepreneurs fail to create and implement a plan? Because they are afraid of marketing and sales, they think marketing is overwhelming, they don't want to be perceived as pushy, and they want people to like them!

What I want for you, by the end of this book, is for you to have no fear about creating and implementing a consistent and effective marketing plan that attracts all the cash and clients you want. I want you to have a plan in place that will mean you know exactly where you are going and you will know how you are going to market yourself every single day. You will know the tools you are going to use. You will know the approaches you are going to take. And, most importantly, you are going to feel very confident about the approach you are taking. Not only that, but your plan will be super creative, colorful, visual, and actionable!

A marketing plan, like the business plan you created in Chapter 3, doesn't have to be a sixteen-page document. It can be a one-page plan that includes: this is what I am going to do; this is how I am going to do it; this is the time frame in which I am going to do it; and this is the investment I need to make to make that a reality.

Having a marketing plan in place will increase your confidence in yourself as a business owner. One of my favorite mantras is that you have to treat your business like a business, not like a hobby. Plans help you move forward as opposed to sitting there, staring at your computer screen, and asking, "I wonder what I should do now?" That question can keep you feeling stuck, scared, and lost. When you sit and wonder what you should do now, you make ineffective marketing decisions, or you choose not to do any marketing at all. You must have a simple business plan to know where you want to go in your business, but it's even more crucial to have a marketing plan so that you know how to attract the clients to get all the business you want.

Marketing Mistake #7 – Relying on only one or two marketing tactics to market your business.

Relying on only one or two tactics to market your business is like eating only one or two types of foods day after day: soon your body won't be getting the nutrition it needs. A robust marketing plan is one that includes a variety of tactics. In Chapters 10 through 15 we will go over many different marketing tactics so that you can choose the ones that will be most effective for getting you in front of your specific audience and that will also be the most fun for you. I am a big believer that we don't have to try to do everything and that marketing can be fun.

One of the things I often hear from creative entrepreneurs is that they rely strictly on word-of-mouth to build their business. While this is certainly a wonderful marketing tactic, it's one that you have no control over and it is severely limiting. At some point, this stream of marketing will dry up, and you will find yourself wondering where all your clients are. Referral marketing is an important tactic, but it should be just one of many tactics you implement to grow your business.

Another marketing tactic that creative entrepreneurs rely on too heavily, especially the shyer ones who don't like networking or speaking in public, is social media. I'm not going to get on my soapbox right now, but you cannot build your business by relying only on tactics that are free or by thinking you can have the freedom and flexibility you dream of by hiding behind your computer.

My goal with this book is to help you with three things: your money mindset, your marketing mindset, and your marketing matrix. I will help you build a group of tactics that will effectively use the strengths that you have to create a magnetic marketing plan that attracts cash and clients consistently. We're going to spend a lot of time on that in the next few chapters, so I'm not going to spend more time here talking about tactics. Just be assured that I will walk you step-by-step through the best ways to market your business—online and in person.

Marketing Mistake # 8 – Not having a follow-up system in place.

Creative entrepreneurs struggle with systems and with structure. They prefer to have a business that flows from their creative genius and doesn't require them to be tied down. Sadly, this hits creative entrepreneurs where it hurts the most—in their wallets. I talked in earlier chapters about how not having money systems in place can hurt your bottom line, but here I am talking about leaving money lying on the table in plain sight. One of the secrets to being a successful entrepreneur is to have multiple automated systems in place for following up religiously with your prospects.

Remember how I described that we want to market to 67 percent of the people who are a maybe and not just the 3 percent we want to market to right now? It takes time and effort to do this effectively. You have to nurture the relationship. I think creative entrepreneurs make two mistakes here: first, they are afraid to be salesy or pushy, so when they get a "maybe" or a "not right now," they let the client go; and second, because they are disorganized, they don't have a system for consistently following up with clients.

Let me give you a more specific example of what I mean by failing to follow up religiously. Let's say speaking is one of your favorite marketing tactics, and you love to talk about nutrition tips for raising healthy kids. You are speaking to a group of parents at a local preschool who are all concerned about raising healthy kids or they wouldn't be there. Suddenly, you have an entire room full of people who are leaning in—they liked what you had to say, and they want to learn more. Many of them probably come up to you following your presentation and ask a lot of questions, and you are delighted to stay and answer every single one because you are passionate about your topic and about helping these parents.

However, the mistake creative entrepreneurs make is believing that if they get in front of their specific audience and share great information, those people will somehow remember to call you when they really need you. Remember that only 3 percent are looking for an urgent solution to their problem. The other 67 percent are interested in learning more but maybe don't have a particular problem right now. Remember, people don't care about you; they care about themselves and their Three Ps (pain, problems, predicament). You might have touched them for a moment, but if you failed to create a follow-up system to stay in touch with those prospects, you have lost them forever. You must have a system in place that will enable you to take them from being just a person sitting in that room to being someone with whom you can follow up and continue to build a relationship.

Here are three examples of systems that can help you follow up religiously with your prospects and continue to nurture your relationships with them, without feeling like a used-car salesman

1. In the scenario above, you could have a system for getting people onto your mailing list so that you can follow up with them using an e-mail newsletter or autoresponder system. How do you collect their e-mail addresses? Offer to give them

an additional free report, a recipe booklet, or a checklist they can use right away. In exchange for the free gift, you ask for their e-mail.

2. Imagine that you spoke to a room of twenty parents and five of them handed you their business cards and asked you to please follow up with them. You drop those business cards into your purse or briefcase, go home, and forget about them for a week or two. By the time you follow up, it's too late. The person has already found another solution to their problem—yikes! Create a simple system for yourself for following up with people you meet, whether you are speaking, networking, or standing in line at Starbucks. Where could you put those business cards so that you would not forget to send a follow-up e-mail or make a phone call? One suggestion would be to make sure that at the end of each day, you ask yourself, "Was there anyone I promised to follow up with today?" Don't go to bed until you have done it!

3. There are two other systems I want to mention here for following up religiously with your clients: spreadsheets and what is called CRM (client relationship management) software. The type of business you are in and the number of people with whom you are trying to follow up will determine which system will work for you. I prefer a simple spreadsheet. You can see a sample in your

companion workbook of what a system might look like for following up with the people you meet.

Marketing Mistake #9 – Spending too much time trying to get their marketing right rather than get it going.

I think this mistake is especially true for creative entrepreneurs who tend to be perfectionists and are hypercritical of their own work. When creative entrepreneurs start their business or decide to launch something new, they spend so long trying to get their marketing perfect that they never get it going. If you are not marketing, you are not making money. Clients will ask me, "Is my logo right?" My response? "Nobody cares about your logo—go get a client! Why are you stuck on your logo? What problem does that solve for your specific audience?" Your marketing collateral can be irrelevant if you are not making money.

Let me share an example of the impact this can have on your business. Remember the story about Julie, the graphic designer? Julie was sitting on her website and not taking any action. She didn't want to do any marketing because she didn't like her website and didn't want people to see it. If she hadn't waited to perfect her website before marketing her business, her life and her earnings would have changed dramatically. Because she didn't have her website updated, she didn't want to do networking, and she didn't want to send out mailers or do anything that might allow people to see what she considered to be a less than perfect website. Julie didn't do any marketing to get new clients for four or five months. No marketing equals no new clients and no cash flowing in. She experienced a big dip in her income during the first quarter of the year because she refused to take action. One new client usually means anywhere from $1,000 to $10,000 a year for Julie. Yikes!

Moving forward without waiting for your marketing collateral, website, speech, or whatever to be perfect is a secret that successful creative entrepreneurs know. "A body in motion stays in motion" applies to your business, not just to physics. Get ready to learn simple tactics to help you get into action and create consistent momentum. You don't have to get everything right. You just have to start marketing today. Remember, you have to be a marketer first and foremost and not worry about all the little details. They'll come along as you need them—I guarantee it. I prefer to push myself into implementation rather than into perfection. I hope that you do too. Perfection is not a great marketing tactic. It's time for another mindset shift, and I have a fun, creative way to help you do that.

Create a Marketing Muse!

I invite you to create a Marketing Muse to support you in growing your business. S/he might be your Million Dollar Muse, Prosperity Muse, Abundance Muse, Spiritual Marketing Guide .... You get to decide where you need the most support right now.

You can create this Muse in any format that you desire: collage, clay, paint, crayons, tinfoil, or cardboard. Your Muse can be two- or three-dimensional. Allow your Muse to take whatever form feels most playful and most loving.

Once you've created your Muse, display her where you can see her on a daily basis. Your Muse will serve as your companion as you journey through the rest of this book. Here are several ways to connect with your Muse:

Invite your Muse to write a letter to you, telling you how she can support you best. Ask her what her thoughts are about your business. Write a letter back to her, saying how much you appreciate her guidance and loving support.

Have a written dialogue with your Muse, allowing her to coach you through some of the inner work you will do throughout this book.

Your Muse is there to offer loving guidance and support. This is also a fun, creative way to connect with your own inner teacher and to trust the voice within that knows exactly what to do next.

Marketing Mistake #10 – Creative entrepreneurs like to play it safe.

This mistake goes along with getting it right rather than getting it going. It's more important to get it right, so we play it safe. Does this sound like you? *"I'm going to stand back until I have all the pieces in place instead of jumping out into that scary unknown and shamelessly marketing myself."* I hear this from my clients over and over again. They don't know what to say or how to say it, so they say nothing.

I cannot tell you how many times I have tried to implement different tactics or make offers to my specific audience and have fallen flat on my face. Over and over again, I have tried new tactics, titles, offers, webinars. Each time I put something out there and don't get the response I want, I learn something new about what my audience did or did not want. This allows me to offer something different that does get a great response! This is the infamous "fail early and often" concept. When you're not afraid to fail, you will stay in motion and gain valuable insights along the way.

I love Thomas Edison's famous story about how he perfected the light bulb. Edison failed to perfect the light bulb (one of the few creations he merely refined but did not invent) so many times it took him 10,000 attempts to perfect. However, rather than accepting failure 9,999 times, when asked about his failures, he said, "I have not failed. I have just found 9,999 ways that do not work."

Read more at http://under30ceo.com/how-michael-jordan-and-thomas-edison-failed-their-way-forward/#h8QPgYiDriLbrVu5.99

Being scared of making mistakes forces you to play it safe instead of just jumping out there and making an offer. Woody Allen said, "Ninety percent of success is just showing up." Creative entrepreneurs don't show up because they want to get it right. They play it safe, stay in the background, and never grow their businesses. I'm encouraging you to get over that play-it-safe model. Stop living in the safe zone. Just do it.

Heartfelt Dialogue

Many women play it safe because on some level they are afraid of success or of what they may lose if they start to play a bigger role in their community or the world at large. I invite you now to have a heartfelt dialogue with the concept of success. Imagine that success is sitting across the table from you, enjoying a cup of tea. Take out your journal and answer the following questions from the perspective of success:

- "How do you like living in my world?"
- "How can I help you?"
- "How can you help me?"
- "Who do you wish that I was more like?"
- "How can I improve our relationship?"

- "What would you like to do for me that I'm not letting you do?"
- "What beliefs do you wish I would change?"
- "What can I do to spend more (or less) time with you?"
- "How can I attract more (or less) of you?"
- "What do you wish I understood about you?"
- "What do you wish you understood about me?"

Marketing Mistake #11 – Showing desperation in your marketing.

Creative entrepreneurs often struggle to make ends meet in their business because of many of the mistakes I have outlined so far. There's no money coming in, they can't pay their bills, and they are feeling scared and desperate. Their marketing becomes calling people on the phone or standing up at a networking event and asking, "Do you need me? Do you need me today? I think I can help you today. Do you need me?" They become a sales-based marketer instead of an attraction-based marketer. They push themselves on people, and you can feel it.

I received a phone call recently from someone with whom I did business, asking me if I would renew his service early because he needed to pay his rent. Do you think this gave me confidence in his service? I don't know about you, but I'm never that compelled by someone who is desperate. I don't want to work with people who need me more than I need them. I want to work with somebody who is sought after in their industry and even difficult to get access to. It makes me ask, "What have they got going on? I want some of that, whatever it is!"

One of the ways you may be creating this aura of desperation (which you may not even be aware of) is by undercharging for your products or services, offering deep discounts, or even giving away time and products for free to try to get clients in the door. You are much more compelling to someone who needs help if you are the type of person who has enough business already to support you—or if you at least market yourself that way, even if you are struggling for money. If you are the type who needs my business in order to survive, you are really not someone I want to do business with. I hope you hear that. It may sound harsh, but it's another major mindset shift. Be careful of the language you use to promote your products and services, as well as the tone in which you say it.

Marketing Mistake #12 – Not having a system in place to automate your marketing.

Because creative entrepreneurs tend to struggle with systems, fixing this mistake seems particularly daunting. This is true especially if you are a creative genius at what you do but feel completely overwhelmed by technology and contemporary modes of marketing, such as social media, blogging, webinars, and other online tools. We're going to talk more about this later when we get into the different marketing tactics, but what I want you to be aware of is how to get to the point where your marketing systems work on their own for you and don't require your constant time and attention. I want to help you get your marketing working for you twenty-four hours a day, seven days a week. Creative entrepreneurs are passionate about their lifestyle. I know you value freedom and flexibility. I know you long for more creative time. Automating your marketing is one of the quickest ways to increase your exposure and create more time for play.

Four Marketing Mindset Extras

We've talked about twelve marketing mistakes creative entrepreneurs make in their marketing. Did you identify with some of them or with all of them? Are you beginning to see how shifting your mindset around your role as a marketer is crucial to your financial success? I want to share four additional mindset shifts that I think will help you optimize the marketing you are going to do in your business.

The first mindset extra is to understand and see marketing as a story.

Creative entrepreneurs are great at telling stories and painting visual pictures, but they might not see their personal story as valuable marketing collateral. We become even more attractive to our specific audience when we begin to talk about our story as well as when we use the element of story in what we do.

Notice how I have sprinkled different stories throughout this book so far. Stories make better teachers than facts and figures. A good story is compelling. When I told you about Tom and his brother with the two lawn-mower businesses, did I get your attention? If you tell a story, you are more likely to grab people's attention and keep it. Did you read about my crazy roller-coaster day in Chapter 1? That whole chapter was a story designed to show you that I have been where you are and that I know how hard it is to learn to love money.

Story is an important part of what you offer your clients and your prospects. It gives you a chance to show them what you have done and how it got you to where you are today. Story goes a long way toward establishing you as the expert. One important element of using story is to tell stories about all the people you have helped, served, or changed in some way. Think about how you can turn your clients' successes into narratives or how your personal journey can be shared as more of a memoir than a resume.

You are a hero

Write down the story of someone you have helped. How did you help them? What was the result? How did they feel afterwards? How did you feel?

The second mindset extra is that marketing is a seed mentality.

I think this is so important for creative entrepreneurs to grasp and to remember. What you do today does not affect you tomorrow, but it begins to affect you months from now. If you spend this week doing no marketing, six months from now you will have a gap in your business. From a marketing perspective, what you do today sometimes gives you results now, but often those results appear six months to a year down the road. Remember that our marketing is attraction-based. Not everyone will need you right now. You have to nurture your relationships with your specific audience so that when they do have a particular problem, you are always top of mind.

Part of the reason I try to build a much more complex marketing system for myself is that the more I work in marketing, the more I guarantee my success for six to eight months down the road. I've got this constant stream of people moving toward me who want to use my services. When I don't do that, when I don't plant the seed today, I don't get the result down the road. Develop the seed mentality. You plant the seed today and expect a harvest six months from now.

Idea Box: Draw a cartoon or doodle that represents you planting seeds and reaping the harvest. What seeds need to be planted? What type of harvest do you want to reap? What will you do after the harvest?

The third mindset extra is expectation.

Expectation affects reality. What I expect my business to do for me is what it will do. What I expect to happen, does. When I get out and look for clients that are looking for me, they tend to show up for me. Not only is it a seed I plant, but it's also an expectation I have. So, as I go out into my world, I expect that the people who need my business will show up for me. They'll start coming my way if I do the work to make sure they know I exist and that I can solve their problems. If I go out there looking for them, expecting them to show up, I go to my client base with a very different approach.

Again, it's not an approach of desperation; it's an approach of expectation. The prospect who needs me will come and find me. It's almost like my energy becomes an attraction mechanism. It becomes a magnet. When I expect to provide great services and resources for the people that work with me, they start coming my way because they sense and know my confidence in what I do. So, expectation is a critical mindset extra. Expectation means you are clearer in the message you present in your marketing and in your interactions with potential clients.

Finally, trust is a powerful marketing tool.

People do business with us, get involved in our business, and hire us because they know, like, and trust us. One of the things I want to make sure you learn as you read farther in the book is how to build that trust. You might have the best approach to whatever your business is, but if they don't trust you, they will never work with you.

Chapter 9

What Is a Marketing Plan and Why do You Need One?

Throughout this book so far, you have heard me say that not having a marketing plan in place is one of the massive mistakes creative entrepreneurs make. You may agree or disagree with me, or you may be feeling completely dismayed and overwhelmed at the thought of spending days or weeks creating a plan that you don't understand how to implement.

I want to invite you to take a deep breath and relax. Creating your visual, actionable marketing plan will make your creative spirit sing in happiness and delight. I want to take the fear, the dread, and the feeling of being overwhelmed out of the equation and teach you a model for marketing that you can return to over and over again.

What Is a Traditional Marketing Plan?

When you consider the definition of a marketing plan from a corporate perspective, it sounds something like this entry from <u>Wikipedia</u>:

"A marketing plan is a comprehensive blueprint which outlines an organization's overall marketing efforts. A marketing process can be realized by the marketing mix. The last step in the process is the marketing controlling. The marketing plan can function from two points: strategy and tactics (P. Kotler, K.L. Keller)."

This sounds too technical, complex, and—dare I say it?—strategic for the creative entrepreneur who just needs to get clients walking through the door on a regular basis. "Blueprints" sounds like architectural drawings with too many details. I believe that marketing plans for creative entrepreneurs should be one-page long and incorporate only the most important elements to help them attract cash and clients.

Most of us don't enjoy the benefits of a multibillion-dollar marketing budget like Coca-Cola, nor do we have dedicated staff doing all the creative effort and legwork to design and implement a long-term marketing plan. What we do have in our favor are flexibility and time. We have the ability to constantly course correct—to make quick decisions and try new things when one marketing tactic fails to bring in the bucks as we'd hoped. That doesn't mean we don't need a plan; it just means that our plan is flexible.

What does a marketing plan for creative entrepreneurs look like?

Remember how I talked about creating a marketing plan that is attraction-based? When you focus on educating your clients, nurturing your relationship with them, and sharing your expertise by giving away your tips, marketing becomes meaningful. Part of the mindset shift I want you to experience is that marketing can be heart-centered. You have nothing to be afraid of when you approach marketing with an attitude of serving others first.

How are we going to accomplish this? By creating a visual marketing plan that you can relate to and have fun with. While there is definitely some strategy that goes into creating any marketing plan, for the right-brained, creative entrepreneur a marketing plan should simply be an action plan designed to get you clients. To begin, your plan should include a few tactics that you enjoy and that get you in front of your ideal clients! It should combine your financial goals with your to-do list.

Take a moment to jot down the answers to the following questions. This will help you begin to form the core of your marketing plan. You can draw some of this information from your one-page business plan in Chapter 3 as well.

- How many new clients do I need?
- How many new clients do I want to serve this year?
- Who are they?
- What are their biggest problems?
- Where are they spending their time?
- What do I think is going to be the fastest way to let them know that I can help them?

Your marketing action plan should match your financial goals. If you need 100 new clients, you will need to create a more diverse plan than someone who wants to find two new clients. Look back at the collage you created in Chapter 4. What do you want to create?

If you are just starting out in your business or you are not reaching your financial goals, **the majority of your time needs to be spent marketing your business!** If you don't have a solid marketing plan in place, you will spend too much time spinning your wheels without taking the right actions. Successful marketing is about consistency and persistence, but that doesn't mean we can't have fun with marketing along the way.

Three Reasons Why Visual Marketing Plans Work Best for Creative Entrepreneurs

There are three reasons why visual marketing plans can lead to more cash and clients for creative entrepreneurs.

1. Not all entrepreneurs are linear or verbal thinkers: combining color, images, and text helps right-brained people convey their thoughts and feelings more easily.

2. Creating a collage of images brings marketing messages to life and shows the holistic nature of marketing. It also allows creative entrepreneurs to integrate all aspects of who they are into their marketing. This is where creative entrepreneurs can have fun with their personal brand. Using visual marketing allows creative entrepreneurs to showcase all of who they are and what they stand for.

3. "What you focus on grows." One reason creative entrepreneurs aren't attracting business consistently is that they are not focusing on the right things in their business. Creating a visual plan reminds them to stay focused on attracting the perfect clients.

If you create a beautiful, visual plan, you are more likely to hang it where you can see it. Seeing your plan daily will remind you of the actions you need to take and will help you stay focused. When you have one of those frustrating moments of feeling stuck or overwhelmed, turn to your marketing plan and ask yourself, "What is one action I can take right now to create some momentum?" Then do it. Still struggling?

Now might be a fun time to have a dialogue with your Muse. What creative inspiration can she offer?

Visual marketing plans allow you to see your goals in a creative, fun way that uses ALL your brain, not just your left brain. Visual marketing plans are like high-definition television: they bring everything into clearer focus. Thinking about marketing from this perspective gets your creative juices flowing and sparks new ideas, beliefs, and areas for growth.

Are you making this mistake in your marketing?

Before I tell you about my color wheel marketing theory and how to make marketing fun and effective, I want to introduce another major mindset shift. I have been teaching marketing to entrepreneurs and small business owners for over ten years. For many of them, marketing is intimidating and overwhelming. Business owners also find marketing frustrating when they feel as if they are not seeing a return on their investment. You can imagine how difficult it was for me to sell an ad to someone who felt like advertising didn't work for them and was just a waste of money.

I often heard comments from people such as:

- "Nothing is working."
- "Advertising is a waste of money."
- "I don't have any money to invest in marketing."
- "I have tried everything, and I don't know what else to try."

- "Why should your solution be better than anyone else's?"

Does one or more of these comments sound familiar? Do you feel like you're struggling to understand marketing and create a plan that works? If you're frustrated and disillusioned with the results you're seeing from your marketing, it could be because your perspective on creating marketing content is skewed.

Marketing content or collateral includes everything from your website to your business card and your Facebook page. The mistake that creative entrepreneurs make in their marketing is to create marketing content that is "me-focused" rather than "client-focused." Remember that our goal is to create marketing that is attraction-based, not pushy or salesy. To do this, all your marketing collateral needs to focus on the problems you solve and the results you create for others.

Here are a couple ways to help you recognize if your marketing is "me-focused":

- Your business card has a laundry list of all the services you provide; for example, a printer might list all the different types of printing they can do for you.
- Your brochure is full of all the features of your business but doesn't mention any benefits; for example, a coach lists all the different types of training they have received and the tools they use to help people but not any of the problems they solve.

- Your website doesn't say anything about who you serve or the problems you solve for them; it just repeats the laundry list of services, features, and tools along with all your training and certifications.
- You don't focus on building relationships or educating clients about how you can help them. You aren't actively engaging in conversations with your clients through social media, networking, or blogging; you are just trying to sell them your latest product or service. An example of this is the blogger who uses every post to try to sell something. They don't offer any helpful tips or try to educate their readers. They are just repeatedly pushing out the next offer. This pushy blogger then shares their sales pitch on all their social media sites, probably annoying anyone who follows them. There's no relationship, no education, and no heartfelt connection.

Creating a successful marketing campaign requires yet another major shift in your mindset. Most of us go into business because we have a valuable skill or tool that we want to share with the world. We see ourselves as experts at helping people, and often we are passionate about helping as many people as we can. So our marketing tends to focus on "ME," what I as the business owner do best and how I do it using all the different tools, tactics, and skills I have learned along the way.

But the truth most business owners don't understand or value is that people don't buy the tools you use. They do buy YOU when you are being very clear about how you can help them. Remember that your prospects are looking for specific solutions to their Three Ps—their pain, problem, and predicament. Understanding the problems your clients most want to solve is the secret to marketing success. This is why you have to shift your marketing mindset from "me-focused" to "you-focused."

How do you accomplish this? It's time to define your attraction-based marketing plan. I know I said that nobody cares about your business, and I want to remind you that your first layer of marketing has to be other-focused. Once you have attracted people in, then you will want to show them why you are the perfect solution to their problem.

Chapter 10

Color Wheel Marketing Theory for Creative Entrepreneurs

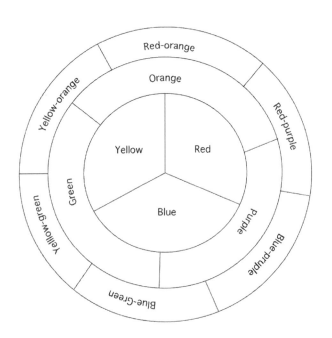

In every basic art class, students are introduced to the color wheel as a quintessential tool for designing, crafting, and creating beautiful works of art. The first color wheel was created by Sir Isaac Newton in 1666 and has been used by both scientists and artists ever since. Do you remember your color-wheel basics?

Let's do a quick review of the color wheel. The color wheel is comprised of three types of colors—primary, secondary, and tertiary. We could also talk about warm and cool colors or complementary or analogous colors. I am not here to go into any great detail about color theory, but I do want you to see how the color wheel can serve as a visual reminder and powerful analogy for how to construct a marketing plan that works. A comprehensive marketing plan, like a color wheel, should include a variety of tactics that create harmony and wholeness.

Wouldn't it be great if marketing were like a color wheel and you could just spin the wheel to find the most profitable combination of marketing tools to create your perfect marketing plan? Well, you can! But first, you need to know a few things about your business goals and about marketing in general.

If you are a creative entrepreneur who struggles with traditional business planning and marketing strategy, you will love this creative visual planning! Together we are going to craft a marketing plan that is fun, focused, and unique to you.

In this chapter, I will focus on what I call the primary colors of a great marketing plan.

If you remember your art lessons, the primary colors are red, yellow, and blue. Together these three colors contain the seeds of everything you need to know to create a vibrant marketing plan for your business. Just as there are three primary colors that combine to form all other colors, at the center of every great marketing plan, there are three key pieces of information that all have to work together to create a perfect synergy. Out of this synergy will flow your passion, your lead generation, and your success as a creative entrepreneur.

The Primary Colors of Marketing

For me, those three essential nuggets of information are represented by the primary colors on the color wheel, like in the image below.

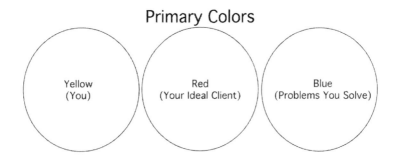

Primary Colors

- **Yellow represents you and your unique gifts!**
- **Red represents your ideal client.**
- **Blue represents the problems you solve for your ideal clients.**

By the end of this chapter, you will have a clear vision of exactly how to fill in the primary colors on your color wheel. By answering a series of questions and getting your crayons or markers out, you will begin to construct your personal Color Wheel Marketing Plan™. Let's start with yellow.

Yellow = Your unique gifts

Our unique gifts are not our training or the tools that we use. They are not the name of the school we went to or the famous people with whom we have studied. Our unique gifts are often defined by how others see us and by the specific way we see, help, serve, and nurture our ideal clients in ways that create powerful results for them. Sometimes our unique gifts also involve our big WHY that we discussed in Chapter 3.

No matter what industry you are in or what kind of work you do, no one else does it quite like you do. Look at the following list. Which of these apply to you?

- Your friendly smile that pulls people in?
- Your ability to listen?
- Your intuition and empathy?
- Your ability to solve a problem quickly?
- Your ability to ask questions?
- Your enthusiasm?
- Your curiosity?
- Your quick wit?
- Your vision?
- Your ability to move others to action?

If this stumps you and you can't answer these questions, dig deep into your well of courage and go ask—ask your spouse, friends, and, in particular, ask your clients what they love most about you. Be amazed and accept their answers with a simple thank you. Now own those gifts and add them to your color wheel.

I recently did this myself as part of my own color-wheel process. I asked several of my favorite clients to share three words they felt described me. It was hard to ask, but I'm glad I did. Here's what a few of them had to say: *amazing, brilliant, knowledgeable, creative, inspiring, nonjudgmental, organized.*

In the last chapter, remember how we talked about not playing it safe? This is a great time to step out and ask for some help from the people in your life who already know, like, and trust you. And yes, your parents count, too.

Here are a few more questions to help you get clear about your unique genius:

- What are you great at?
- What do you love to do?
- What would you love to get paid to do?
- What do you love to do even if you never get paid for it?
- What do others say is your genius? (see questions in previous section)
- What makes you different from others in your industry?
- What is your personal story?

These are just a few of the questions you can answer to create clarity around your unique genius as a business owner. Forget about your certifications and qualifications; those are the tools you use to do your job, but they are not what makes you unique.

Why does the color yellow represent you?

We won't spend too much time on color theory, but for those of you with inquiring minds, I will address the connection between color and different elements on the wheel. If theory isn't your thing, feel free to skip this section and go straight on to reading about red and defining your ideal client.

I intuitively chose the color yellow to represent your unique gifts because of its brightness and ability to shed light from the insight out. I didn't even think about why I chose yellow or red or blue in the beginning. I introduced my color wheel marketing theory on my blog last summer. One of my regular readers asked if there was an intentional connection between the colors and the elements of marketing. Being a creative type who adores idea-storming, I decided to explore the connections. I'm glad I did.

Color psychology is definitely not my field of expertise, but I do think introducing a bit of meaning here will add

some depth to the color wheel. I also know how creative you are! Don't like my color choices? It's your color wheel, so feel free to make it any colors that are meaningful to you! Color psychology certainly plays a very strong role in branding and the creation of marketing collateral. Why shouldn't it have an impact on creating our marketing plan?

Here is a brief description of the color yellow from the website Empower Yourself with Color Psychology. I scoured several websites and books on color psychology and found this site to be the most comprehensive in its descriptions. If you are interested in exploring color psychology, start there. You will find a link to this website in the footnotes.

> ***The color yellow is of the mind and the intellect.*** This color relates to acquired knowledge. It is the color which resonates with the left or logic side of the brain stimulating our mental faculties and creating mental agility and perception. Yellow is creative from a mental aspect, the color of new ideas, helping us to find new ways of doing things. It is the practical thinker, not the dreamer. Yellow is the best color to create enthusiasm for life and can awaken greater confidence and optimism. Yellow is related to the ego and our sense of self worth, to how we feel about ourselves and how we are perceived by others.

Interesting, right? Yellow stimulates the part of our brain that allows us to be creative and successful in our business. It's perfect for learning to honor and acknowledge our gifts and deciding how best to share them with the world. It's also related to ego and our fear of how others perceive us.

Remember that your unique gifts can help temper the ego and tap into your brilliance!

Red = Your ideal client

Knowing who your ideal client is and where to find them is a key piece of any business plan, not just your marketing plan. Yet I find that all entrepreneurs, not just creative entrepreneurs, resist narrowing their focus to a particular niche or type of person. Why do they resist? Because they are afraid that if they narrow their focus, they will have even fewer clients flowing in than they do now. Nothing could be farther from the truth! I know it seems counterintuitive, but trust me—the narrower and more specific your focus, the more clients can self-select and say, "Yes, you have exactly what I need right now!"

I talked more about why you need to define your ideal client in the last chapter. This section is devoted to how to create an ideal client profile. Trust me—once you do this, your marketing will feel so much easier! Trying to market to everyone is overwhelming and creates chaos for you and confusion for people in the marketplace.

Here are a series of questions to get you started. You could get out a journal and start writing down your ideas. You could doodle images that represent your clients, or you could create a mind map to begin creating a visual representation of your perfect client.

You could also start by picturing one of your favorite current clients in your mind. Answer the following questions as if you were talking about one specific person.

- Who are they?
- What are their biggest challenges?
- What are their pains, problems, and predicaments?
- What do they love?
- What do they believe?
- Where do they shop?
- What are their hobbies?
- What is their age?
- What kind of relationship are they in?
- Do they have kids? pets? gardens?

It's crucial that you create a very detailed profile of the one person that represents your perfect client. You want to include their psychographics (the study and classification of people according to their attitudes, aspirations, and other psychological criteria, especially in market research) as well as demographics and geographic location.

Here are a few more questions to ponder about your favorite client:

- What makes this person your favorite client? Include every detail you can think of! Some examples might include the following: they are smart, creative, pay on time, have a great sense of humor, are punctual, authentic, etc. You get where I'm going with this.
- Where does your favorite client hang out, both in real life and online? What types of groups, associations, and organizations do they participate in? What social media sites do they use?

Once you have a clear mental image of your client, I want you to create a detailed, written profile and visual image as well. In the last chapter, I talked about how important both expectations and trust are. The more clearly you can define your perfect client, the easier it will be to attract more of them.

Why does this work? First, you know exactly with whom you want to work, and you expect to work with them. Second, you know them intimately, making it easy to establish a relationship with them based on trust.

Meet Sheri: A sample ideal client profile

Here is an example of a very detailed ideal client profile. See if you can see all the information that I asked you to think about: Who is she? What are her problems? Where does she spend time?

Dr. Sheri Williams is a forty-five-year-old, well-educated, successful entrepreneur with two school-aged children.

She has been married for close to twenty years. She works full-time and has been in the same career field since college but started her own business only a few years ago. Starting her own business has been so much more challenging than she ever thought it would be. She feels like she has to make too many personal sacrifices just to keep her business going. She is feeling stuck, frustrated, and overwhelmed by all the details of taking her business to the next level.

She loves the work she does and knows she's good at it, but she struggles with the day-to-day routine of running her business: the invoicing, payments, budgets, planning, marketing. She wishes she could just spend all day working with her clients and not worry about the rest.

Her husband has a successful career with a local engineering firm and works long hours, too. She thought owning her own business would be the answer to all their problems, but it hasn't been. She is working harder than ever. In addition to her long work hours, she is an active volunteer at her kids' schools and is on the board of several local nonprofit organizations.

Sheri wishes she had more time to exercise, meditate, and get a pedicure, but she is too busy managing her family's busy schedule along with her long work hours. She can't remember the last time she and her husband took a weekend trip alone or even went out for a date night for dinner and a movie.

Her kids are showing signs of stress, begging her to spend more time with them. She feels as if she has alienated all her girlfriends, having said she was too busy to get together too many times. She doesn't feel as if she has anyone to talk to or that anyone would understand her current challenges. From the outside, it looks like Sheri has it all: financial success; a great husband; smart, good-looking kids; a nice house; two nice cars; and even a boat, which they never have time to use.

By Friday evening, Sheri is exhausted and just wants to sit on the couch with a glass of wine and watch mindless television. What happened to the creative, dynamic woman of her youth? What happened to the mom who loved to play board games and who valued family dinners?

Sheri is feeling out of shape, disconnected, isolated, and depressed. She knows something has to give, but she feels stuck and doesn't know which direction to turn. It doesn't seem possible to make a change right now or to know which piece to give up.

She longs for the freedom and romance of her younger days when she and her husband took long walks on the beach or went camping with the kids on weekends. She misses time spent with girlfriends and breaks from the household chores and busy family schedule. She misses the time she spent writing in her journal and finding quiet time just for herself.

Financial success has not brought her family the freedom or the happiness that she and her husband dreamed of as newlyweds. Now, she looks across the dinner table at her husband and wonders, "Who are you?" She looks in the mirror and wonders the same thing: "Who am I? What makes me happy?" She doesn't know the answer to this question anymore, and she knows it's time to seek outside help.

She is committed to making the necessary changes to get her life and her family back on track before it's too late. She wants to have it all: a romantic relationship with her husband, time with her kids, and a profitable business that allows for more freedom and flexibility.

Can you see how knowing all of these details about Sheri would make it easy to create marketing messages that would make you magnetically attractive to her? Can you begin to see how easy it is to predict what her biggest challenges are?

The number one reason you are not reaching your financial goals is that you are not clear about who your Sheri is and how you can best serve her.

Once you know the who, you can:

- Target clients who want what you are selling, making sales easier.
- Reach that 67 percent who are a maybe because you are speaking their language.

- Create a website that is juicy and attracts your perfect clients because it speaks directly to them.
- Create a marketing plan that is magnetically attractive to your ideal clients no matter where you meet them, saving you time, money, and tears, trying to sell to the wrong people.

Color Psychology: Why red?

I think red is the perfect color to represent ideal clients. I can see why I intuitively chose this color to represent their passions and their challenges. Red is the energy clients want to create and embrace in their business or in the personal power that they need to reclaim in their lives and relationships.

Here is what Bourn Creative writes about the meaning of the color red on their blog:

> **Red** is assertive, daring, determined, energetic, powerful, enthusiastic, impulsive, exciting, and aggressive. Red represents physical energy, lust, passion, and desire. It symbolizes action, confidence, and courage. The color red is linked to the most primitive physical, emotional, and financial needs of survival and self-preservation.

> **The color red** is a highly visible color that is able to focus attention quickly and get people to make quick decisions, which is one of the reasons fire trucks and fire

engines are usually painted red. Flashing red lights mean danger or emergency, while stop signs and stop lights use the color red to alert drivers about the dangers of the intersection.

Red represents power and courage. The color red is the basis of the traditional red power tie or red suit in business, and the red carpet for celebrities and VIPs. Red's association with courage and bravery makes it a color that is used often in national flags, on shields, and in achievement patches.

Here are a few more examples of why I think red works as a perfect color choice on your mix-and-match marketing plan:

Remember Julie, the graphic designer? She helps her clients show up on the printed page and online as creative, brilliant, and passionate—all energies of the color red that her clients want to embrace but don't know how.

Remember Gloria, the vocal coach? Her clients want some of that yummy red-carpet energy and to feel like a star!

Then there is Cassandra, who owns a yoga studio. Doing yoga leads to more courage, passion, and connection in all areas of our lives—all qualities of the color red.

Learning to harness the power of red and showcase it in our work is an exciting and intentional piece of marketing genius that anyone can employ! The color red is energetically the perfect placeholder for the dreams and challenges of our ideal clients.

Now it's your turn to put some thought into the connection between the color red and your clients. Does the analogy hold?

Blue = The problems you solve

Blue is your sweet spot or the money spot on your color wheel. It's the point where your unique brilliance intersects with the needs of your ideal client. Once you are clear about the problems you solve and for whom you solve them, marketing is simple. All your blogging, social media posts, speaking engagements, and other marketing tactics have a shared intention: to educate your clients about the problems that you are best at solving for them.

Let's take a minute to do a quick, guided visualization. Close your eyes and imagine that you are your ideal client. Take a deep breath. Think back over your detailed profile of this person. See yourself standing in her shoes. Take another deep breath or two until you clearly feel yourself being this person. Now ask yourself: "What are my biggest challenges? What are my most urgent problems? What am I certain that (insert your name here) can help me with?" Once you feel you have enough information, open your eyes.

Grab a notebook. Make a written list of the particular challenges you know your client has and how you have solved those challenges. List as many as you can think of.

Once you are super clear about the biggest pains, problems, and predicaments your ideal client is worried about, you can begin to build your marketing plan and your marketing promise!

Take a look at your list; prioritize the problems you solve. Is there a particular problem that has to be solved first, before you can move on to the next one? Create a sequence of events and determine the starting point for all your clients.

The Meaning of the Color Blue

According to the website Empower Yourself with Color Psychology:

> This color is one of trust, honesty and loyalty. It is sincere, reserved and quiet, and doesn't like to make a fuss or draw attention. It hates confrontation, and likes to do things in its own way.

> From a color psychology perspective, blue is reliable and responsible. This color exhibits an inner security and confidence.

You can rely on it to take control and do the right thing in difficult times. It has a need for order and direction in its life, including its living and work spaces.

This is a color that seeks peace and tranquility above everything else, promoting both physical and mental relaxation. It reduces stress, creating a sense of calmness, relaxation and order – we certainly feel a sense of calm if we lie on our backs and look into a bright blue cloudless sky. It slows the metabolism. The paler the blue the more freedom we feel.

In the meaning of colors, blue relates to one-to-one communication, especially communication using the voice – speaking the truth through verbal self-expression – it is the teacher, the public speaker.

Blue is the helper, the rescuer, the friend in need. It's success is defined by the quality and quantity of its relationships. It is a giver, not a taker. It likes to build strong trusting relationships and becomes deeply hurt if that trust is betrayed.

Wow, talk about being a direct hit when it comes to solving people's problems. Blue is the best color to represent this section of your Color Wheel Marketing Plan™. Blue reflects the feelings and emotions that a dynamic problem solver should convey. Now you know why blue is the color of the power suit and, along with red, is present in the flags of so many different countries!

How do you connect with the color blue? How can you draw on the energy and meaning of blue to lend credibility to your unique gifts and highlight the brilliant way you solve problems for your clients?

Let's Get the Crayons Out

Now that you have all of this information collected on your primary colors of marketing, let's get the crayons out! You will find a blank color-wheel template in your workbook. I encourage you to print it out or draw one of your own. Get some markers, paint, or crayons and color in the three primary colors in the center. Then label them with a few words, doodles, or even magazine images that represent your unique genius, your ideal client, and the two or three key problems that you solve.

The goal of creating a visual marketing plan is threefold:

1. It's more fun for us creative, right-brained entrepreneurs to create.

2. We're more likely to sit down and create it when it's visually represented and playful.

3. When you intentionally design your marketing strategy visually and understand how to structure the information in a way that makes sense to your

creative brain, you will also be able to create an action plan that you will stick to!

I want to do a quick check-in with you. How are you feeling? Are you getting clearer about your marketing? Before you read ahead to the secondary colors of marketing, I want to be sure you take the time to complete this section. As long as you have these three key pieces of information in place—your genius, your client, and the problems you solve—you can build a dynamic and effective marketing plan.

The next two chapters will dive more deeply into all the different tactics you can use to attract your ideal clients and nurture your relationships with them.

Chapter 11

The Secondary Colors of Your Marketing Plan Are All about Strategy!

Secondary Colors

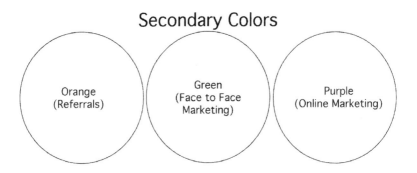

Orange (Referrals)

Green (Face to Face Marketing)

Purple (Online Marketing)

In this chapter, I want to talk about the secondary colors of your marketing plan. Secondary colors are created when you combine two of the primary colors. Do you remember the formulas from grade school?

Red + Yellow = Orange

Yellow + Blue = Green

Red + Blue = Purple

What do secondary colors have to do with our marketing plan?

You need to include some tactics in each section of the color wheel in order to create a comprehensive plan. That doesn't mean that you have to take action on every tactic on a daily or even weekly basis. Some of these tactics are foundational; once they are in place, you don't have to do anything else. Others you might do weekly, monthly, or quarterly.

Secondary colors represent our first interactions with our ideal clients, so they have to be a combination of our primary touch points as discussed in the last section:

- What is your unique genius?
- Who is your ideal client?
- What problems do you solve for that client?

Our first interactions with prospects or potential clients can happen in one of the three following ways:

Orange: Someone gives you a referral – This is the orange section of your color wheel. Orange is a warm color, just like referrals are warm leads. Referrals rock! They are a direct connection between you and the prospect stemming from a personal introduction. Getting more referrals should be an active part of your marketing plan. If it's not, start asking your current clients for referrals now!

A referral strategy is a foundational part of any marketing plan. Once you have a strategy in place, you need to ask for referrals and nurture referral relationships on a regular basis, but probably not daily. A referral strategy can be as simple as asking current clients or other people you know for referrals. It can also be more strategic and involve compensation for referrals. You can offer a financial incentive for referrals—I do! I love referrals and am happy to give my clients and friends a percentage of the income I receive for a referral. I don't have to work nearly as hard to get those clients as I do with other strategies. A warm lead is one that already knows something about you and has an initial level of trust established based on the recommendation of their friend or colleague.

Green: Someone finds you online (your website, social media, guest blog post, podcast, interview, etc.). I call this type of contact a green lead, and it goes in the green section of your color wheel. **Green** is all about growth. There are many shades of green appearing in nature, plus, green is also the color of money, at least in the United* States. But it often takes some effort to turn a green lead into a client.

Your online strategy should be about showing what problems you solve for people and the results you get.

Online marketing strategies are about creating content that makes you attractive by showcasing your expertise and clearly calling out to your clients. Online strategies are about building and nurturing relationships with the 67 percent of the market place that are still a maybe.

Take a look at your current online presence. Reflect on your website copy, your Facebook page, your tweets, pins, and posts. What do they say about you? Does your copy scream, "Me, me, me!" or does it say gently, "I'm here to help—trust me!" When you think about online marketing, remember to think green. Remember what Kermit the Frog always said, "It isn't easy being green." If you are more like Miss Piggy than Kermit, you have some mindset work to do!

Purple: You meet someone in person (networking, speaking, attending an event, or hanging out at the coffee shop are all examples). Let's talk about the color purple.

I love this description from <u>Bourn Creative</u>:

> **Purple** combines the calm stability of blue and the fierce energy of red. The color purple is often associated with royalty, nobility, luxury, power, and ambition. Purple also represents meanings of wealth, extravagance, creativity, wisdom, dignity, grandeur, devotion, peace, pride, mystery, independence, and magic.

Red represents your client, and you want to meet them when they are on fire: ready, willing, and committed to invest in whatever you are offering. Blue represents the problems you solve and invokes calmness, peace, solutions, *ahhhh*. Together these become the inspiration for your purple strategies—getting out and connecting with people!

Your in-person connections must also focus on how you can help people—not on what you do, but whom you serve and what problems you fix best! Here are a couple ways to make sure that you are thinking purple when you are out in the community:

1. Write an elevator pitch, a thirty-second commercial, or a brief introduction that clearly illustrates what problems you solve and for whom you solve them. Here is an example of one of my commercials that I would share at a networking event:

   You know how creative entrepreneurs are constantly chasing bright, shiny ideas but struggle to make enough money in their business? Well, I help them attract cash and clients so that their life is more fun and financially secure, and they have more time to do what they love.

   Notice that I called out the *who*—creative entrepreneurs—and pointed out what the problem is—not enough cash and clients. I did not say how I would do it. I did say what the result of attracting cash and clients would be: more fun, financial security, and more time. My current clients tell me they want more of these things!

2. When someone asks you, "What do you do?" Don't say, "I am a ...." That's not what they asked you. Instead, share how you help people. My short answer is usually, "I help creative entrepreneurs make more money" or "I help creative entrepreneurs build profitable businesses." See the difference? If I simply said, "I'm a business coach," no one would care.

3. When you're invited to speak or present to a group either in person or virtually, make sure that your topic is focused on the specific problems that your ideal clients most want solved. If I had titled this book *Color Wheel Marketing Theory*, would you have bought it? Probably not! Your title and your content have to focus on solving the problems your clients most want solved.
Here are a few examples of titles that will attract more people by showing specifically what problems the speakers address:

   - 3 Massive Mistakes Professional Women Make That Keep Them Overwhelmed!
   - Three Huge Mistakes We Make Leading Kids ... and How to Correct Them

- Fill Your Workshops ... with EASE! 3 Massive Mistakes Workshop Leaders Make that Keep Their Event Rooms Empty!

I can hear you now thinking to yourself, "But that sounds cheesy or salesy. I don't want to mislead people." Remember Chapter 5 and the mistakes creative entrepreneurs make? One of the biggest mistakes you can make is not touching on the pain that people feel and offering a solution. In each of the titles above, the authors touch on a particular pain point and offer a solution in their content. Your most important goal is to turn that 67 percent of the market from an initial "I'm interested" to an "I'm buying now!"

How to Avoid Feeling Overwhelmed by Marketing

We have just added three new areas and a number of possible marketing strategies to our color wheel. Marketing is about picking a few key strategies at a time to try, not about doing them all at once. So let's take a minute and pick the secondary marketing strategies that feel the most fun and the most effective for connecting with your ideal clients.

Grab your journal or a blank sheet of paper, and ask yourself the following questions. In the next chapter, I will go into greater detail about the different marketing tactics that will help you implement your strategy, but you can start making note of what feels most fun to try.

Be creative and have fun with this; there are no right or wrong answers.

1. Orange Strategy: What is my best opportunity for getting referrals now?

2. Green Strategy: Where are my ideal clients hanging out online? What would be the most fun and effective way for me to connect with them online?

3. Purple Strategy: Think like royalty! Where can I show up in person as the leader and expert in front of my specific audience?

You will need to have at least one tactic in each of these three strategic areas. You have a blank template in your companion workbook, or you can draw your own. I encourage you to get it out and start filling in your visual marketing plan with color and text that represent your preferred strategies. Remember to make your marketing plan visual and enticing! I want you to fall in love with it, and I want you to look at it every day as your visual reminder to take some marketing actions daily.

Chapter 12

The Tertiary Colors of Your Color Wheel Marketing Plan

Are you taking the time to work through your Color Wheel Marketing Plan™? If not, I encourage you to do so now. Reading all the books on marketing in the world won't help you if you don't take action, even though I know marketing isn't always fun and at times seems like a big, confusing muddle.

I can empathize. I'm definitely a right-brained, creative entrepreneur who has struggled with structure or seeing things in a linear fashion. I came up with this solution because so many of my clients dread talking about marketing strategy and planning. It feels overwhelming and exhausting. There's no guarantee it will work, and they don't know where to start.

My clients are the reason I developed this concept of the marketing plan based on a color wheel. The idea was initially inspired by a class I took on color theory. We were asked to create a color wheel using collage. You can see a sample of that collage in your companion workbook so that you can enjoy the full range of color. It was a fun project, and I loved how the colors flowed into each other, but the challenge was to make sure that the primary colors were clearly defined and stood out from the other colors. Primary colors are the core of everything—in art and in marketing. It is the blend of colors that makes each color wheel unique. In the world of art, artists and designers define this as their personal palette, and these colors are easily recognizable in their art. Do they tend to use pastels, vibrant colors, contrasting colors, or neon colors?

It is the tertiary colors on a marketing wheel that allow us to play with the blend and create our personal palette of marketing strategy.

Do you remember what the tertiary colors are on a color wheel?

The tertiary colors combine a primary and a secondary color. This is when art and marketing start to get more fun. You still have to start with the primary colors, but now you get to start playing with different marketing tactics, blending colors and strategies that make sense for your business and work for you.

This sample color wheel shows all three layers of colors.

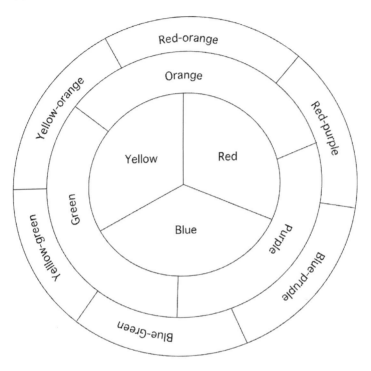

Take a deep breath. All those colors might be starting to feel a bit overwhelming. It's pretty easy to start filling those spaces with marketing tactics and tools, isn't it?

Here's the trick: When you stay focused on your primary colors, the mixology makes more sense. When you feel overwhelmed, go back to the center of the color wheel. Remember that our secondary colors were about how we initially connect with our prospects. The tertiary colors look more closely at the psychographic and demographic details of our prospects to understand more about who they are and where they are spending their time. The secret to marketing success and to profitable lead generation stems from two key elements: defining your target audience and understanding what its challenges are.

Here are the tertiary colors by name and type of tactics:

- Red-orange: One-on-one referral tactics
- Red-purple: Attending other people's events
- Blue-purple: Hosting your own events
- Blue-green: Online tactics such as a website, blogging, webinars, video
- Yellow-green: Social media tactics using sites like Facebook, Twitter, and Pinterest
- Yellow-orange: One-to-many referral tactics

Bear with me now. Keep breathing. We're going to go through each of these sections in more detail. I will also remind you that this book is about strategy and planning. I'm not here to help you design your Facebook strategy or teach you how to blog. I'm here to show you why focusing on a broad but not infinite number of marketing tactics will help you attract cash and clients—fast!

Red-orange: One-on-one referral tactics

Red emphasizes who your ideal client is, and orange is your referral strategy. On a marketing plan, this would equate to the specific tactics you use to generate more referrals. This might include tactics such as:

1. Asking existing clients for referrals on a regular basis.

2. Attending networking events where you will get referrals from other business owners. People mistakenly believe networking is about selling to the room of people you are in front of. True networking is about getting to know people and trust what they do so that you can send them those lovely warm leads and receive leads in return.

3. Building referral partnerships with other entrepreneurs and business owners who target the same market as you. For example, a mortgage broker and a real estate broker are great referral partners who might share an ideal client: first-time home buyers. Perhaps you are a graphic designer. A great referral partner for you would be someone like me who focuses on strategy, not design. Another great referral partner would be a wholesale printer who doesn't have an in-house designer and wants to refer their printing clients out.

Your marketing should include all three of these referral tactics, but take your time. Start with your low-hanging fruit. Ask your current clients or business relationships for referrals. Help them by being extremely clear about who you are looking for. You are not looking for referrals to any warm body with a checkbook. You are looking for a specific client with a specific problem that you can solve.

Over time you will naturally begin to build additional types of referral tactics through your networking and connections in your community, both online and offline. Start by making a list of what type of business owner would make a great referral partner for you. Whom do you know already, and whom would you like to meet?

I will share an example of a friend of mine who implemented this strategy with incredible success. I met Claire a couple years ago at an awards luncheon. We sat together, and I felt an instant rapport with her. Claire is a financial planner who recently left an upper-management position to build her own financial advisory team. She is brilliant at engaging people. Joseph, her business partner, is brilliant at engaging numbers. Her job is business development, which means marketing and bringing in potential new clients that choose to have Claire and Joseph manage their finances.

When my husband and I were looking for a financial planner, there were two things that Claire did that made her stand out from other financial advisors and led my husband and me to hire her team to take care of our investments. Firstly, Claire built a relationship with me and shared with me her vision of her business and who she was looking for. She did not try to "sell" me or even invite me into a sales conversation. When Brad and I started interviewing people, Claire was at the top of my list because we already had a relationship. My husband and I felt that not only were we choosing them, but they also were choosing us. They were very clear about who they wanted to work with. This ensured that we were a good fit and that we were more likely to have a sense of loyalty and send them referrals.

Secondly, Claire also shared that she had personally met with hundreds of potential strategic partners such as lawyers, realtors, CPAs, bookkeepers, and others who would be able to help her clients with all their needs related to money. She carefully selected a handful that shared both her team's core values and the same ideal client profile that she and Joseph had created. She has nurtured those relationships over time and can, in full faith, refer her clients to any one of these partners, knowing they will take care of them as well as she herself would. You can imagine that each of these partners feels the same about Claire and will send their clients to her. This is a mutually beneficial relationship that puts the needs of the client first but ultimately benefits the bottom line for all parties concerned. I appreciated this strategy from the perspective of marketing, but it also increased Claires's value to me personally. Brilliant, right? I know that as we need estate planners, tax planning, and other financial advice, the referrals from Claire are as reliable and trustworthy as she is.

I cannot think of a better way to do business. In fact, one of my biggest regrets when we moved to Santa Barbara a couple years ago was the loss of all my referral sources. I was well known in my previous community for being a go-to resource when you needed a referral. I would get calls for plumbers, mechanics, chiropractors, and once, even someone looking for an expert on dinosaurs to talk to a local Boy Scout troop. Guess what? I did know someone who could talk about dinosaurs, and I had reliable referrals for all the other resources, too. I actively worked to build connections with experts in my community. For the eleven years that I owned my business in Texas, I never felt like I did business with a stranger. Either I knew someone to ask for help, or I knew who to ask for a referral. When my accountant moved to Dubai with her husband, it was stressful to think about having to find someone new. She knew my business and our personal finances inside and out. But guess what? I knew three other accountants that I could interview and that I trusted to take care of our taxes.

I encourage you to consider who you know and to think about who you want to meet so that you can start building a solid network for one-on-one referrals in your community. You can do this both in person in the city where you live and online with experts you are connected to.

Building and maintaining potential one-on-one referral relationships is a key marketing strategy that must have a place on your Color Wheel Marketing Plan™. Go ahead and color this section in on your wheel now and add a few names of people you are already connected to or would like to reach out to in order to build your referral network.

Red-purple: Attending other people's events

The red-purple tactics involve connecting with your ideal client and showing what problems you solve. In this section of your color wheel, you will focus on doing this in person by attending events hosted by other people.

Here are some suggested tactics for connecting with people. Remember that I'm not asking you to do all of them. I am asking you to pick one that you like and commit to doing it this week! Also, add two or three of these tactics to your Color Wheel Marketing Plan™. Later I will show you how to create an effective action plan to make sure you're implementing these tactics.

Reminder: When you attend these events, do NOT talk about what you do; rather, tell them how you serve others! People only care about how you can help them; they don't care what techniques or tools you use. Practice your elevator pitch before you go so that you will be able to confidently answer their questions. Focus on the RESULTS you have created for other clients.

Types of Events to Attend

1. Attend networking events like chambers of commerce, leads groups, associations, Meetup groups*, or other places where like-minded business owners spend their time. Spending time with other entrepreneurs is a great motivator. You can learn from them, share woes with them, and create your referral partnerships.

* Meetup is an online social networking site that supports people with shared interested in getting together offline. It's a great resource for finding people to connect with in your community. Learn more at http://www.meetup.com

2. Speak at events like the ones mentioned above— local conferences, Rotary groups, corporate lunch-and-learns, etc. Speaking is one of the fastest ways to establish your expertise and get in front of a group of your ideal clients. This is a much faster way to attract cash and clients than just talking one-on-one with people. Terrified of public speaking? I'm going to say this now, and it will sound cruel to some of you—get over it! I was terrified to speak in public when I started my business. I would be sick to my stomach, and my face would turn beet red, but I kept doing it and kept getting better at it. Speaking was one of the best ways that I was able to grow my readership and increase ad revenue for my publishing company! Consider Toastmasters or other groups that help you gain both confidence and experience with public speaking.

3. Attend other people's live events, workshops, trainings, conferences, association meetings, etc. The goal is to connect with your potential audience where they spend time. I can guarantee you they are not all hiding behind their computers. Where are they? Go find them, meet them, ask them questions, be a great listener, and share how

you might be able to help them. Remember that you are attending events to build relationships, not to sell to the room. Be heart-centered, be curious, be open.

4. Have coffee/tea with at least one new person a week. This goes hand-in-hand with our previous strategy. You don't know what people need, who they are looking to help, or how you might be able to help them unless you care enough to sit down and have a conversation.

5. Attend a Meetup group that is focused on something you and your ideal clients love to do, even if it has nothing to do with your business. Love to hike? Eat out? Go to museums? Watch movies? Play board games? Make art? Walk your dog on the beach? Chances are there are many others who share your interests. Go meet them! You might be surprised how many clients you can attract in this seemingly random way.

You might struggle mightily with this category on the wheel, but the truth is that to grow your business, you have to get out and meet new people. You can't hide in your studio or office, hoping people will stumble across your website. I'll repeat, *You can't hide in your studio or office, hoping people will stumble across your website.* That's not a model for success.

Are you beginning to see the layers come together? As we build out the color wheel, we want to start to add the colors and strategies that work best for us and are most effective in targeting our ideal client.

Now it's your turn again. Add the next layer to your color wheel. What one or two red-purple tactics are you willing to try?

Does this theory really work?

When I was initially working on the Color Wheel Marketing theory, I had a powerful brainstorming session with a client about an event she was preparing to host in the near future. She wasn't sure if she wanted to do it or how to market it. She knew that if she didn't have at least ten people participate, it would not be worth her time financially. She also knew that if she cancelled, she would let down a couple of her clients who were looking forward to the event.

I shared the Color Wheel Marketing concept with her and how I felt it applied to her situation. I discovered during our conversation that she wasn't clear about her unique brilliance or her ideal client and the problems she could solve for them. She was not feeling committed to the event because she had so little clarity about why she was doing it, for whom she was doing it, or how it would benefit them. By the end of the call, she had more clarity and was able to make some decisions about what she needed to do next.

Here's what Kathy had to say after this session: "In our conversation, Minette brilliantly guided me to the core of what I want to do. She masterfully asked questions so I uncovered my perfect niche and helped me translate my ideas into a tangible benefit for my ideal client." Ultimately, Kathy decided not to host this event based on our conversation and her clarity around who she really wants to work with in her business.

Yellow-orange: Your one-to-many referral strategies

Let's talk about the yellow-orange segment on your marketing color wheel: it is about building strategic partnerships. These are different from the referral relationships we discussed in the red-orange section. One way these tactics are distinct is that they often occur virtually rather than in person. Remember that yellow is about knowing your unique brilliance. When it comes to building strategic partnerships, your partners will want to know what makes you special. Why should they partner with you?

Some of the strategies for connecting with either referral partners or strategic partners are the same. For example, sharing core values and an ideal client profile are important to building great strategic partnerships.

There are three types of virtual strategic partnerships that I want to address in this section:

1. Creating connections with other creative entrepreneurs who serve the same audience you

do and co-creating a virtual event such as a webinar or teleseminar.

This might also include being invited to speak to someone else's specific audience or participate in a telesummit. The idea here is to increase your exposure to your specific audience by connecting with people who are also targeting the same audience.

For example, my online business manager and I co-created a strategic partnership in 2014. We both love working with creative women entrepreneurs, but we don't offer the same services; we just target the same specific audience. In fact, I often refer my clients to her to help them implement their marketing strategy. We created a Biz Gift Giveaway and invited other entrepreneurs who all target women entrepreneurs to share a gift. The gift was either an educational video or an audio book or e-book that our ideal clients could download and get instant tips for building their business. The Biz Gift Giveaway had several purposes: to bring great new content to our existing audience in areas where we can't help them, to build our list by attracting new clients who want what we are offering, and finally to expand our network of like-minded entrepreneurs by helping them build their list and become a trusted resource for our clients. It's what I like to call a win-win-win.

2. The second type of strategic partnership is to create an affiliate marketing plan.

Affiliate marketing is where you invite other people to promote your products, and they get a percentage of what they sell. It also works in reverse—you find a product that you love and are willing to promote to your audience through an e-mail marketing campaign and/or a social media campaign. When done well, affiliate marketing is a win-win for both parties. The trick is to do business only with people you know, like, and trust.

Affiliate marketing can be a great way to create quick revenue if you have a solid e-mail list that trusts you and knows you will share only credible resources with them. You can often sell a product without having to personally know the person or people who created it. For example, I am a big fan of GetResponse.com, an e-mail service provider. I often promote this service to my clients who are just getting started with e-mail marketing. I could sign up as an affiliate and make money anytime someone buys this service using my affiliate link. I don't know the creators of GetResponse.com, but since I have been their customer for several years, I feel confident referring them to others.

3. Finally, the third type of strategic partnership is also called a joint-venture partnership.

If you wonder how all the seven-figure business owners are making so much money online, this is how! These are reciprocal relationships where two parties agree to promote each other's products. This is a very simple definition of a complex process. I would encourage you to start small by connecting with others in your industry and inviting people into strategic alliances where you are co-promoting each other's work. It's a powerful strategy if you have a virtual business and are selling info products, home-study programs, or coaching programs. This is not a strategy that will work for every business.

The goal of yellow-orange is to put relationships in place that help you increase your exposure to many of your ideal clients so that the leads are pouring in rather than merely trickling in.

Here are some questions to ask yourself about strategic relationships and your marketing plan:

- How are you using these strategies currently in your business?
- If you are not using these strategies, how might they work in your industry?
- Do these strategies make you go, "Huh? I don't get it"?

- Are you scared to reach out and talk to other entrepreneurs?

As you build out your personal Color Wheel Marketing Plan™, it's inevitable that some doubts, fears, and questions will arise. Right now, take a deep breath and remember we are in the planning phase. Anything is possible at this point, so just have fun dreaming about having a steady flow of clients from your existing relationships and current clients.

It's time to pull out the paints, colors, or crayons and start playing with your marketing plan again! What yellow-orange tactics will you add to your color wheel? Keep adding colors and concepts, ideas and tactics to your color wheel as you go. Commit to implementing one new or familiar tactic at a time.

If you are feeling confused and overwhelmed, let's connect. I would love to offer you a complimentary strategy session where I guarantee you will connect to your marketing plan with more clarity and more enthusiasm! I offer only a few of these sessions each week. You will find information at the end of this book on how to schedule one of these sessions.

Yellow-green: You and social media

I personally love this segment of the color wheel, but I have to be careful not to spend too much time and effort here. Remember that the primary colors for creating yellow-green are yellow and blue. You can use social media to share your unique brilliance by showing what problems you solve and the results you have created. You can also use social media to share educational content that established you as the perfect expert for solving certain problems.

Social media may seem like an unknown entity or like a rabbit hole into which people frequently disappear, not to be seen for hours at a time. I know I have been guilty of getting lost in Pinterest; following one fantastic pin after another is much like following a trail of bright, shiny ideas. The dialogue in my head goes something like this: "Ooh, I could do that. Must save that recipe to try later. Ha! That cute kitty picture made me laugh out loud— must show Maggie. ... Now, what was I looking for?" Does this sound familiar?

Perhaps you enjoy social networking sites for personal use, but you haven't attempted to use social media as a strategy for growing your business. As a creative entrepreneur you might find using your social networking sites for marketing offensive, worrisome, or overwhelming. Are you thinking right now that all your friends on Facebook will unfriend you if you start trying to sell them something? Remember that our aim in this book is to create a marketing plan that makes you magnetically attractive! *Social media* is defined by Wikipedia as "the *social* interaction among people in which they create, share or exchange information, ideas, and pictures/videos in virtual communities and networks." I love the simplicity of this definition and the reminder that social networking sites create opportunities for us to share, connect, and exchange ideas, inspiration, and—yes!—offers to help!

Social media can be an invaluable part of a marketing strategy for creative entrepreneurs when used appropriately. There are four things to know about using social media as part of your marketing strategy.

First, you need to understand that social media is a slow-growth strategy, not a quick way to attract cash. The best use of social media is to build relationships and to create a tribe of followers who know, like, and trust you.

Second, social media is an excellent way to connect with your ideal clients, but the focus must be on nurturing relationships with your specific audience. One way to do this is to solve some of their problems in real time by answering questions, sharing your best tips, or giving away free content.

Third, social media is just like Meetup: people tend to follow one or two sites, not all of them. You don't need to have a presence on every social media site in existence. Pick the ones you enjoy and where your clients are spending time. An inactive Facebook page or Twitter account will not show you as an expert.

Finally, you have to create a consistent presence to get noticed. This means that posting, tweeting, and sharing have to become part of your weekly marketing activities. You can automate this process using tools like Hootsuite or hiring a virtual assistant to disseminate your content, but you still need to personally engage and connect with your followers.

We are going to talk about scheduling your marketing time in a later chapter, but I want to assure you that a social media strategy does not require you to spend hours a day on Facebook and YouTube. Usually one to two hours a week is more than enough!

Knowing Your Ideal Clients Should Drive Your Social Media Choices

Now is a perfect time to review the center of your color wheel and to remember who your ideal clients are and what problems you are solving for them. What social media site is your specific audience most likely to frequent? Here are a few key demographics from Pew Research Center and Business Insider about some of the most popular social media sites. This information will help you determine where your ideal clients spend time online.

Demographics of the Most Popular Social Networking Sites

- 74% of online adults use social networking sites.

Percentage of adults using social networking sites by age:

- 89% of young adults ages 18–29
- 82% of adults ages 30–49

- 65% of adults ages 50–64
- 49% of adults ages 65+

Which sites are they using?

Contrary to popular belief, **most people** *aren't* **using multiple social networks.** Most use just one site.

Facebook is by far the most popular platform with 71 percent of online adults using this social networking site.

- 19% of adults use Twitter, and it is most popular with those between the ages of 18 and 29.
- 17% use Instagram, and it is also popular with the younger crowds.
- 21% use Pinterest, and more women than men frequently use Pinterest.
- 22% use LinkedIn, and more men than women use LinkedIn regularly.

Facebook and Instagram have the most engagement, with users frequenting these sites on a daily basis.

LinkedIn is notable for its highly educated and professional audience. If you are targeting corporate clients or entrepreneurs, many of them are actively engaged on LinkedIn. The age demographic tends to be older as well, with their highest concentration in the 30- to 49-year-old range.

YouTube reaches more adults ages 18 to 34 than any single cable TV network. I know this is true for my two teenagers. They are more likely to watch a YouTube video than to turn on the television.

I want to encourage you to pick one social networking site to begin promoting your business. Already using social media? Are you spending time on the right site? Remember that your social media strategy should flow from the center of your color wheel. The purpose of social media as a marketing tactic is threefold:

1. Establish you as an expert by sharing content that is educational and/or inspirational

2. Make sure you are getting exposure with your ideal clients

3. Showcase the specific problems you solve for those clients

10 Tips for Becoming a Social Media Superstar

Each social networking site is unique and involves a particular strategy for being seen, heard, and shared. Those strategies are beyond the scope of this book, but here are ten tips to make sure that you are using social media effectively. You can also download my free report, "21 Ways to Be a Social Media Superstar" at http://www.mindfulpatterns.com/artful-marketer-book.

Showcase your creativity. Writing, art, drama, makeup, recipes, dance ... what shows off your creativity?

1. Be authentic. Don't be afraid to share all of who you are! Think you are kind of quirky? Be quirky! Love poetry? Share poems! Dress like a gypsy? Show it off!

2. Get graphic. Use images, photos, and colors to highlight your messages.

3. Get comfortable with video! Video is one of the hottest social media tactics on the market right now.

4. Share your best stuff. I mean it! You are an expert, so let people know it. Create great content like checklists, tip sheets, inspirational quotes, training videos, or audios and e-books that appeal to your specific audience and help them solve their most urgent problems.

5. Make it easy for people to share your amazing content. Add share buttons to your website.

6. Make it easy for people to connect with you on social media, and let them know where you hang out. You can put this information on your website, business card, or in your e-mail signature.

7. Follow other people you admire and share their outstanding content. Sharing great content by others increases your credibility. Comment on their content and invite them to connect.

8. Engage with your audience! Ask questions, have contests, and invite them to the party, chat, or live event. Respond to their comments and connect personally with them.

9. Have FUN! If it's not fun and creative for you, you are not likely to commit to doing it regularly. Brainstorm a list of ideas right now on how you can make social media more fun for you!

What's it going to be? Facebook? Twitter? Pinterest? LinkedIn? Grab your color wheel and add your yellow-green segment. What do you need to do or learn next to be successful on your chosen social media platform?

Blue-green: Beyond social media

Did you know that *blue-green* has been a Crayola crayon color since 1949? I love statistics like this because they make marketing and art fun. Who doesn't love a brand-new box of Crayola crayons?

In the last section on yellow-green, we talked about using social media as a valuable tactic for creative entrepreneurs. The use of the primary color yellow put more emphasis on showing off your talents and unique genius. Remember that all your marketing flows from the center of the color wheel. With the color blue-green, the emphasis shifts back to blue, with just a touch of yellow, and remember, blue represents the problems you solve for your clients. Some of the best ways to do this involve blue-green tactics like blogging, visiting other people's sites and commenting on their posts, following other experts you admire and letting them know what you like about them, or sharing advice and insights in groups, forums, and online chat rooms such as Facebook and LinkedIn. These blue-green marketing tactics, combined with your social media strategy, will work together to attract a steady stream of people to your business.

Cue the parrot, a beautiful blue-green macaw that is repeating the mantra of this book: "Marketing is not about you, but about your clients and their Three Ps." Can't you just hear that macaw over and over again, squawking "Pains, Problems, and Predicaments. Pains, Problems, and Predicaments"?

How many websites have you visited where all the website owner did was describe themselves and talk about how great they were? They didn't say anything about who they work with or how they could help. They just offered a long, tedious list of features showing off their training or tools they used. They didn't say anything about the results these tools would create for you. I bet within a few seconds you clicked away from that website in search of someone who was talking directly to you! Go now and look at the homepage of your website. Is it attractive, or is it me-focused? Here are a few websites that I think do a fabulous job of being attractive and clear about who they work with and what problems they solve:

http://kendallsummerhawk.com/ – Coach for women entrepreneurs http://www.melodyehunter.com/ – Branding expert for empire-building entrepreneurs

http://www.habitat.co.uk/# – furniture and home décor with a lifestyle twist

http://janedavenport.com/ – artist and educator

http://leoniedawson.com/ – coach and mentor for creative entrepreneurs

"But I'm an artist," you might be saying. "I have to show my work!" Well, of course you do, but how you position your work is important. Whether you are a painter, writer, editor, graphic designer, or business coach, showing examples of your work is important, but how you talk about it is what makes it attractive to the 67 percent. Take a look at Jane Davenport's website. What do you notice? I feel invited to play, and I feel welcomed in a place that I know will be creative. It calls out to my creative spirit of play and whimsy. Keep exploring the site. There are plenty of offers to play, to buy, and to learn. It's a great example of educating and inviting me to join her tribe.

In the case of a painter, showing the techniques and processes you use and talking about your favorite brand of paint or where you traveled to capture the images you are painting invite people into your world. I have a friend, Carol Steinberg, who is a painter in Los Angeles, and she does a great job with her blog posts. She paints some beautiful still lifes and often shares where she gets her inspiration. One day she painted two different perspectives of some flowers she bought at the local farmers' market. She posted both online and invited people to vote on which one they liked best and why. She was creating community and engagement with her followers. All the paintings she posts are for sale, but she rarely just posts a painting and says, "Hey, buy this." She tells us the story that makes us want to buy the painting! She not only shares this information on her blog, but on Facebook as well. "Create once then share everywhere" is my motto for marketing online.

Your blue-green marketing tactics include content-creation opportunities such as:

- Creating an FAQ for your website
- Writing a biography of who you are and why you can relate to your ideal client
- Your blog posts
- An e-mail newsletter
- An online magazine
- Comments on other people's blogs
- Interacting and sharing advice and ideas in forums, Facebook groups, and LinkedIn groups.

This section of the color wheel is all about content. Freely share what it is that you know how to do well! Don't be stingy with your content or with your creativity. Don't waste time being humble or modest or thinking your advice doesn't have value. Someone out there needs to hear what you have to say! Give away, share, post, or tweet lots of fabulous online content that showcases your expertise. This is one of the quickest ways to build your credibility with others and to make that "know, like, trust" factor occur more quickly. It's also much more effective than giving away your time as you can help many more people.

The recipe for both social media and other forms of online marketing is to share at least three-parts content to one-part sales. Don't forget about the sales! You have to tell people what you are selling for them to be able to buy from you, but you can do it in a way that is educational, creating a win-win scenario where even if they don't buy now, they are getting valuable content from you.

In this section of your color wheel, think about which of these tactics makes the most sense for you. Keeping your website fresh, attractive, and up-to-date is an ongoing project but not a daily one. Blogging is something that I personally think every creative entrepreneur should add to their marketing plan. Why? Because writing one blog post or article per week can generate enough content to fill all your other marketing tactics. Remember that you don't have to be a great writer to start blogging, just a competent one. Also, if you struggle with writing, use images, art, cartoons, or video in your blog. Invite others to be guest bloggers on your website or interview experts and share your interviews on your blog. Here's a sample flow chart of how a blog post can be repurposed for the rest of your marketing and be used to drive a steady flow of traffic back to your website. Once you have people on your blog, you can tell them what to do next: sign up for your free product and your e-newsletter, buy something, connect with you on social media, or contact you directly.

Blog Post Flow Chart

How one blog post can increase traffic and generate content for a whole week on social media

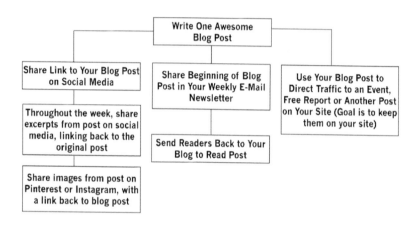

Blue-purple: Public speaking

Which leads me directly to the final tertiary color on our color wheel, blue-purple. The blue-purple section, similar to the blue-green section, requires that you educate your clients about how to work with you and how you can best help them. The difference is that I want you to get out from behind your computer and educate people face-to-face.

I know for some of you this section may cause fear, panic, and the desire to run and hide! Take a deep breath. There are many forms of public speaking, and perhaps one of them will feel right for you. The red-purple section of your color wheel also included some public speaking, but often at other people's events. In the blue-purple section, I want you to consider also hosting some of your own events.

Speaking is one of the fastest ways to grow your business—no matter what business you are in! You get to decide if your desire to attract cash and clients is bigger than your fear of appearing in public. I completely empathize with how painful it is to stand up in front of a room feeling nervous, sick to your stomach, and afraid of looking silly, stupid, etc. I've been there. I used to get so nauseous from nerves that I couldn't eat for hours before a presentation. "Practice makes perfect" is one adage that I adhere to. The more often I got up and spoke in front of a group, the better I got at it. I still get nervous when I speak, and most people I know who do a lot of public speaking say they also get nervous before an event, even if they have been speaking for years!

Here are examples of how you might use public speaking in your business. All of these events are ones that you personally create, market, and fill in on your own or with your strategic partners.

- **Free Self-Hosted Events:** you invite people to listen to you speak in a public venue with the goal of offering content and selling people into a program, workshop, coaching program, or other service. This would work well for artists who invite people in to see their work and learn more about their craft. It would also work well for graphic designers or interior designers who want to share some do-it-yourself tips with potential clients. You might be wondering how sharing DIY tips can get you clients. Doesn't it just encourage people to do it themselves? Yes, sometimes, but more often than not, people realize how much work and expertise is involved—or they fall in love with you and your particular style of design. These events are intended to attract new fans who will become clients, if not now then at some point in time.

- **In-Person Paid Workshops:** you offer educational content based on a specific topic that solves a certain problem for your clients. For example, I could do a three-hour workshop on just Color Wheel Marketing or Learning to Love Money. Other ideas would be art classes, jewelry making, stress relief or meditation, movement, writing—anything to do with your business that you can teach others how to do for themselves.

- **Home Parties:** you invite a small group of people into your home, offer great content, and then offer them the opportunity to join a paid workshop, coaching session, event, etc. This is a great lead-in to the paid workshops suggested above or to retreats or other ongoing programs. Alternatively, you could ask a client to host a home party for you and invite their friends/colleagues to hear you speak.

- **Hosting Live Events:** you host a two- or three-day live training event with the goal of selling people into a longer-term, group coaching program. This is a very popular model in the coaching industry.

- **Live Retreats:** you host at either a hotel or a retreat center in your community, in a larger city nearby, or even in exotic locations around the world. Retreats tend to be smaller and more intensive than live events. People will pay well to attend an exclusive retreat. The retreat model works well for artists, coaches, healers, therapists, or educators. You could spend a whole weekend on copywriting or business planning just as easily as you could spend a weekend teaching art and yoga. Be creative and don't assume a particular model won't work for you.

As I told you in my introduction, I have been a successful entrepreneur for close to fifteen years. I have already built one six-figure business and am currently building my second one. Speaking has been a key part of my marketing success. If I can do it, so can you. Speaking has been the best way for me to get in front of larger groups of people all at once and give them a taste of who I am.

You can learn only so much about me (or anyone) from reading what I write or share in a book, blog post, or social networking site.

Let me tell you about my client Cyndi Elliott. Cyndi is an occupational therapist by trade who is passionate about stopping the labeling of children with disabilities and helping the world to begin to see them with different abilities. Part of her brilliance is being able to see a child's ability and use that ability to help them grow, make changes, or be successful at home and school. Cyndi's passion also stems from her loving and beautiful relationship with her brother David who has Down syndrome. Cyndi published a book called *I See Ability*. This is also the title of her keynote presentation and the name of the movement that Cyndi wants to create in the world. The beautiful book is a collection of photographs of clay dolls that Cyndi created to represent all the different abilities of children with whom she has worked. The dolls capture the essence of playfulness and creativity that she sees in her clients.

Cyndi's challenge was understanding how this book could become the focal point for a marketing campaign and a global movement called "I See Ability." One of the pieces of marketing collateral that we were working on was what I call a "speaker sheet." This is a one- or two-page flyer that promotes Cyndi as a speaker. She will send this speaker sheet to conferences and organizations that would be interested in her "I See Ability" message. When we started working on the content, all of Cyndi's language was me-focused and too technical, plus no one knew what the "I See Ability" movement was about yet. We went through the process of identifying how to turn Cyndi's ability message into one that educators, therapists, and parents would want to listen to.

I loved Cyndi's attitude and willingness to work through her resistance to marketing language. Once she understood that she needed to speak so that others could hear her and show how listening to her presentation would help them solve a problem now, she got it! Her speaker sheet focuses on showing what specific problems her presentations will solve for her particular audience and emphasizes that they will learn tips and tools that they can put into action immediately. Cyndi's passion and enthusiasm for her work are boundless. She is an engaging and dynamic speaker, but that doesn't matter unless she can first get people's attention by educating them about how she can help them.

In contemplating these different public speaking strategies, which one would you be willing to add to the blue-purple section of your color wheel? Just one! Add it to your color wheel now.

Your color wheel should be looking quite full and colorful at this point. Now that you have all of these ideas, what do you do next? How does this color wheel help you create a consistent and effective marketing plan? In the next chapter, I'm going to show you how to take the information on your marketing plan to create an action plan and marketing calendar that will be simple and fun to implement. Once you have a consistent plan in place and you commit to taking daily action, cash and clients will begin to flow in on a more regular basis.

Chapter 13

Time-Management Tips for Creative Entrepreneurs

By now, you should have a beautiful, colorful, and complete Color Wheel Marketing Plan.™ Each segment of the color wheel should have something written on it. Maybe you have added images, too. Feel free to embellish it with glitter glue, stick-on gemstones, Washi tape, or other pretty baubles that make it more appealing to your eye. Perhaps you would like to add an inspirational quote or two around the sides? It's your plan! Remember, you will display your Color Wheel Marketing Plan™ where you can see it on a daily basis, so make it eye-catching!

But just hanging your Color Wheel Marketing Plan™ on the wall will not get you where you want to be. You have probably had some mindset shifts at this point and decided that you need to implement some new marketing tactics if you are going to attract the cash and clients to reach your bold money goal.

Have you struggled in the past to consistently implement a plan? Are you feeling overwhelmed and a bit afraid, knowing you need to make changes but you aren't sure where to start? This final chapter of the book will allay your fears and help you design an action plan that works for your creative brain. But before we get started on your plan, I want to debunk a couple myths that I believe will help you with the mindset required to be a successful marketer.

Myth #1 – Work-Life Balance Is Possible

I was at a workshop last year called "The Courage to Lead." The workshop was based on the teachings of Parker Palmer. I'm a huge fan of his work, and his teachings have deeply changed my perspective on how I approach my career and my life, as well as the subject of work-life balance. In his book *A Hidden Wholeness: The Journey Toward an Undivided Life*, Parker Palmer shows how we have been living divided lives. He writes:

> Afraid that our inner light will be extinguished, or our inner darkness exposed, we hide our true identities and become separated from our own souls. We end up leading divided lives, far removed from our birthright wholeness.

The divided life comes in many and varied forms. To cite just a few examples, it is the life we lead when:

- We refuse to invest ourselves in our work, diminishing its quality and distancing ourselves from those it is meant to serve
- We remain in settings or relationships that steadily kill off our spirit
- We hide our beliefs from those who disagree with us to avoid conflict, challenge, and change
- We conceal our true identities for fear of being criticized, shunned, or attacked

My knowledge of the divided life comes first from personal experience. A "still, small voice" speaks the truth about me, my work, or the world. I hear it and yet act as if I did not. I withhold a personal gift that might serve a good end or commit myself to a project that I do not really believe in. I keep silent on an issue I should address or actively break faith with one of my own convictions. I deny my inner darkness, giving it more power over me, or I project it onto other people, creating "enemies" where none exist.

I pay a steep price when I live a divided life, feeling fraudulent, anxious about being found out, and depressed by the fact that I am denying my own selfhood. The people around me pay a price as well, for now they walk on ground made unstable by my dividedness. How can I affirm another's integrity when I defy my own? A fault line runs down the middle of my life, and whenever it cracks open—divorcing my words and actions from the truth I hold within—things around me get shaky and start to fall apart.

Source: http://www.yesmagazine.org/issues/healing-resistance/a-life-lived-whole

What studying Palmer's work has taught me is that until I feel that my life and my work are fully integrated, I won't be happy or achieve the success I claim to want. I will continue to chase dreams and ideas. I will always be on a quest for meaning outside work rather than creating a meaningful career that allows all of me to shine.

Focusing on integration has allowed me to settle in and stay focused on my current career in a way I was never able to achieve with my last business. And ultimately, it has helped me make peace with being a creative entrepreneur and the challenges that creates in the world of traditional business. I cannot be other than who I am. I cannot separate the wife, mother, artist, marketer, and coach. I cannot ignore or avoid the parts that make me uncomfortable, like taxes and planning. I have to learn how to trust myself to do them my way.

Creative entrepreneurs often avoid what doesn't feel like fun or feels too hard. They sink back into their comfort zone when they don't understand how to do something and refuse to try. I have a client who has been resisting setting up QuickBooks for her business for close to a year now because it feels daunting, scary, and overwhelming. Yet taking this one action will save her time, allow her to outsource her bookkeeping, and likely save her money on her taxes because she will be paying closer attention to her finances all year long. She doesn't want to pay someone to help her; she thinks she has to figure it out on her own, which adds to her fear and frustration. The truth is that she doesn't have to learn all about QuickBooks. She needs to find someone she trusts to help her set it up, teach her how to do a few simple things, and then manage the rest of it for her. The creative entrepreneur's resistance to asking for help and stubbornly believing that we have to do it all by ourselves makes it impossible to grow and sets us up for living the divided life Palmer describes above.

When the creative entrepreneur finds herself feeling stuck and overwhelmed, she feels out of balance, and her priorities are often skewed away from what is most important to her. In the case of the client above, when she is feeling divided, she hides, avoids her problems, and focuses on working harder on what she can manage. She feels ashamed, yet her fear stops her from taking action.

I invite you take a moment to examine your own life. Do you feel divided? Or are you at a place in your life where you are embracing integration? Perhaps you are somewhere in between? In the next section, I'm going to share with you a quick checklist to assess how integrated your life is with your work.

Now, remember that I said that I would debunk the myth of work-life balance? I don't believe that "balance" is possible. I think it's a myth that there is some perfect world where everything in our life gets equal amounts of attention. That's an unrealistic perspective. I do believe in integration and in making time for what matters most.

The life of the creative entrepreneur is more like a juggling act. Because we love to do so many different things, we often juggle many different roles—and we love all of them. We find our attention being pulled in too many directions. When we do drop one of the balls, blame and self-judgment often stop us from moving forward. There is a super funny video on YouTube about juggling by comedian Michael Davis Ford. Listen to his banter as he juggles a sword, a hatchet, and an axe. Learning to add a touch of humor to our juggling and to let go of blame and shame can get us back into action.

I love the juggling of the many different areas of my life, but I notice that when I'm distracted or divided, I start to drop too many balls. Sometimes I drop all the balls and collapse in front of the television with a glass of wine and the cat on my lap. Usually some downtime and a good night's sleep are enough to get me back on track.

Mindfulness Tip: When you start to notice that you are dropping too many balls, take a five- or ten-minute time-out. Sit quietly and take several deep breaths. Allow yourself to be present in the moment. Take out your journal and write down three to five things that you feel grateful for right now. After you write them down, read them aloud or silently to yourself and say thank you. Then, ask yourself, "What is one step I can take right now to get back on track?" Write it down and then go do it. Trust your intuition, even if you hear something like "Take a walk," "Doodle," or "Dig in the garden."

Lifestyle Balance Checklist

Below, you will find a series of statements about the current state of your business and your life. Answer the statements with "always," "sometimes," or "never." Take a moment to acknowledge and celebrate the good habits you already have in place. This list is not intended to be comprehensive. It's intended to be a snapshot of the most important balls that you need to keep juggling.

As you go through the list, notice how you feel about each statement. If a negative thought comes to the surface, acknowledge it and let it go. It's just a thought, not a reality. Nothing on this list is impossible to establish in your life. Pay special attention to the statements that you have resistance to. Again, just notice them and ask yourself, "Why am I feeling so much resistance?"

Life-Work Balance Checklist

☐ I regularly set goals, plan and prioritize - on a daily, weekly, monthly and long term basis.

☐ I have consistent structures and systems in place to support me.

☐ I practice good time-management skills and am diligent with my calendar.

☐ I regularly take holidays, long weekends, time off.

☐ I have a clear line between home and work, even if I work at home.

☐ I ask for help when I need it.

☐ I am good at saying no to projects or people that take too much time and energy.

☐ I am okay with good enough versus perfect.

☐ I get regular exercise.

☐ I eat healthy foods.

☐ I enjoy a regular spiritual practice.

☐ I reward myself for my success!

☐ I am positive, passionate and enthusiastic - every day!

Reflecting back on your responses, notice any trends. Are you doing a great job of taking care of yourself at home but avoiding work? Are you so focused on work you have forgotten you have a personal life?

Life Work Balance

Take out your journal or some blank sheets of paper. Grab some markers or your favorite pen and let's dig a little deeper into your experience of balance. You will find the checklist above and the questions below in your companion workbook. You can download them

http://www.mindfulpatterns.com/artful-marketer-book and print them out.

What is your **TRUTH** about being out of balance? Pick three areas from the checklist that you would like to improve and answer the following three questions for each statement.

- What is the **IMPACT** of being out of balance in this area, and how it is affecting your life and/or your business?
- What is the most powerful **DECISION** you need to make?
- What is one **ACTION** you will take and by when?

Let me share a specific example of how using this information worked with one of my clients. Cynthia had been working with me for a while and had experienced some big a-ha moments in her business. She definitely had the illusion that she was working hard and never had enough time. Perhaps the biggest a-ha was that she had been running her business like a hobby rather than treating it like a business. Cynthia owned a petting farm. She was also an animal educator and would take her animals to preschools and elementary schools to present programs to the kids. Plus, there was animal care that needed to be done early in the morning. Her mornings tended to be busy. In one of her moments of insight, she noticed that she would get work done in the morning, but by noon she might just go collapse on the couch. Cynthia was not spending any time at all on her moneymaking activities, calendar, or planning for her business. It was the classic story of working *in* her business, not *on* her business. Doing this activity helped Cynthia acknowledge where she was out of balance and create a new time-management plan that allowed her to get more work done and still take a midday nap to recuperate from her early mornings. Because of a few small shifts, she was not only happier and taking greater pride in her business, but she also doubled her income in thirty days.

Cynthia's story illustrates how your perspective on time management impacts your business growth and profitability. If you aren't aware of how you spend your time or where you feel out of balance, divided, or disconnected, then adding marketing to your already full schedule will feel overwhelming. And while you probably did the fun part of the work, creating your Color Wheel Marketing Plan,™ you might be thinking it would be easy to stop here. Please don't stop now. While I don't believe that a perfect ideal of balance is possible, I do know that focusing on what matters most to you can bring you more satisfaction and joy along with financial success.

Myth #2 – I Don't Have Time for Planning

Are you constantly saying, "I don't have enough time. I'm too busy. I wish someone could help me manage my time." That seems to be a constant theme with my coaching clients. Their biggest concern is not having enough hours in the day to get everything done. The thought of adding more to their already full schedule completely overwhelms them. To help them be more productive, I have come up with several time-management tips that work for creative entrepreneurs.

Before I share these tips, I want to show you some ways that you may be wasting time or underestimating time. I call these your time-eating gremlins. We all have them, those things that take up our precious time, interrupt us, and stop us from being as productive as we say we want to be. We can't figure out why we never have any time. Our calendar doesn't look that full, does it? These gremlins are the reason that creative entrepreneurs think they can't manage their time. Time management is not the real problem; it's just the symptom.

Time-eating gremlins lurk everywhere

Here are some possible gremlins that may be eating up your work time—especially if you are an entrepreneur working from home. Add your kids, spouse, and the dog begging to get walked to the mix, and this list grows exponentially.

- Underestimating how much time a project will take
- Checking your e-mail constantly
- Jumping onto social media every time you get a notification
- Watching television two or more hours a day
- Letting paperwork and bills pile up
- Doing laundry or other housework instead of making sales calls
- Meeting with people in person instead of by phone or Skype
- Wasting time looking for things (keys, kids' shoes, the overdue bill, or the permission slip for today's fieldtrip)
- Spending too much time on volunteer activities

The list of activities that can distract any entrepreneur is endless. Because creative entrepreneurs tend to avoid or ignore the work they don't want to do, these time-eating gremlins make great distractions. Over and over again I see creative entrepreneurs not making their marketing or other moneymaking activities a priority during prime work hours.

Sometimes there is fear underneath those distractions, in which case we tend to create more activities and make ourselves busy so that we don't have to focus on what is or isn't working in our business. Fear of making sales calls can have us scrubbing floorboards instead of picking up the phone.

In order to manage your time, you have to first manage your mindset and your expectations. It takes a high level of belief, desire, and commitment to be a successful entrepreneur. How badly do you want it? Are you 100 percent committed to making money, or are you creating distractions because of lack of clarity, doubt in yourself, or fear of success? These are very real fears, and I have dealt with all of them at various times in my career. I still struggle at times to get all the pieces of family and business flowing in harmony—I have two teens and life can get pretty chaotic. My husband and I both work from home, and there are endless tasks to be taken care of.

How do we do it when it's all working well? We have our priorities in the right order.

Remember the balance checklist in the last section? Remember the actions you committed to? You have said those are your priorities, but they won't happen if you don't write them into your calendar.

In the past year, I have implemented two specific time-management skills that have had a huge, positive impact on my business. They are time blocking and learning to live by my calendar. I have also taught these skills to each of my clients. But before we get to those two skills, let's talk about to-do lists and priorities.

Why To-Do Lists and Sticky Notes Don't Work

Well, maybe a few sticky notes ... we can't eradicate them completely, can we? In fact, I will show you a fun way to use sticky notes in your planning in another section. But right now it's time to tear up your traditional to-do list. You know which one I'm talking about, right? The one that's several pages long and includes a mish-mash of business and personal to-dos. "Pay the gas bill" is right below "call the vet" and right above "return a potential client's phone call." I have many clients who get downright panicky when I tell them that they need to tear up their to-do lists. They don't believe they can function. They start freaking out about all those balls they are juggling.

What most of them don't realize is that their exhaustive to-do lists are actually limiting their productivity. I'm not saying that the individual tasks are not important; I'm saying that the traditional to-do list is dysfunctional and doesn't work for creative entrepreneurs.

You may not even use a to-do list, preferring to scribble notes on any scrap of paper at hand, allowing these scraps to float, stack, disappear, reappear, and get lost. You probably find yourself spending way too much time scrambling to find your notes and not enough time actually doing whatever was on the sticky note.

Are You Queen of the To-Do List?

If it is helpful to sit down and write out one master list of everything you want to accomplish for the week, make time to do this type of planning once a week, either on a Friday, Sunday, or first thing Monday morning. Make it fun. Grab a giant sheet of paper and some markers and get all your to-dos out of your head and onto one sheet of paper.

Make sure to look at your Color Wheel Marketing Plan.™ What are you committing to this week? Don't add everything on your wheel to your to-do list at the same time. Pick one or two new strategies to implement each week. Like diet and exercise, marketing is a habit. Master one new habit before adding another one.

When this is complete, you will need to prioritize your list. I'm going to walk you through a process for how to do this. Once you get the hang of this, it will go quickly and you won't need to take as long to do it in the future. You will also understand why not every single task needs to go on your daily to-do list.

Your Daily Big Six

One of the reasons that your life feels out of balance and you feel like you never have enough time is that you are not focusing on your priorities. During this process, we are going to create a to-do list that has no more than six items on it. Yes, I just said "six." This is the secret to productivity, time management, and balance, all rolled into one simple system.

If you implement this process daily, I guarantee it will change your life.

First, go through your list and be brutally honest with yourself about each item on the list. Ask yourself these five questions:

1. Am I ever going to do this? (Especially for that item that shows up week after week, such as finishing a book, a painting, or a home-repair project.) If the answer is "no," take it off your list.

2. Could I ask someone else to do this? (Kids, spouse, another family member, etc.)

3. Could I pay someone else to do this?

4. Does this have to be completed by the end of this week?

5. Will this move me closer to my goal or farther away? (This works for business as well as personal to-dos.)

Second, grab your markers or pen and start crossing off any items that you are not going to do yourself or that will not move you closer to your goals. Put a big colorful star or check mark by the ones you are committed to doing this week. Put another symbol beside the items that can wait until later.

Third, add any new items to the list that might come up because of your new perspective. For example: hire someone to finish painting the bathroom; hire someone to help me with my taxes.

Fourth, look at the list carefully and start to prioritize by day of the week. Take into account both your personal and professional to-dos. Pick the six you commit to doing on Monday. Commit to yourself that you will get them done before you go to bed! If six feels like too many, pick five or three. It's not the number that matters; it's the commitment to getting them done.

What successful entrepreneurs and CEOs understand is that each day will be full of distractions, interruptions, and unexpected tasks. By putting only a few items on your must-do list each day, you are creating time and space for the messiness of life. Because creative entrepreneurs are easily distracted by those bright, shiny ideas, the phone call from a friend, or the invitation to lunch, it's vital to your business success that you commit to making some progress every single day.

How Do You Know Which Six to Pick?

I would look at your long list and pick the most urgent first. That would mean items that have deadlines attached. "Pay a bill" or "call the dishwasher repairman" might be at the top of your list on the personal side, along with "finish a proposal for a new client" and "make three sales calls" on the business side. Notice how simple each of these items are. While they might seem small, each of them keeps your home running and cash flowing into your business.

Then, I would add items from your work-life balance list. Perhaps you commit to walking for an hour three days a week. Perhaps you need to spend an hour planning your marketing goals for the week or month ahead.

I don't put appointments on my to-do list. I put action items, tasks that I must accomplish regardless of time spent with clients, colleagues, etc., on my to-do list.

Finally, what are your biggest goals for the year? What can you add that will move you forward? Again, this can be personal or professional.

The point of the big six is to focus on what will create momentum and keep you on task and on track. When we create an overwhelmingly long to-do list, we often don't know where to start, or we spend time focusing on activities that don't help us move forward in our business. Remember our time-eating gremlins? To-do lists are another form of a time-eating gremlin.

I would encourage you to create your big six a week at a time, knowing things might change and will need to get moved around. Flexibility is the key to a balanced life. One of the aspects of being an entrepreneur that I love most is my ability to course correct mid-stride. I have goals, I know what I want and need to accomplish, but I am also flexible enough to be able to make quick changes.

Here's what a sample couple days might look like for me.

What do you notice, other than I didn't list any appointments?

Monday:

- one-hour walk
- put dinner in crockpot
- write copy for newsletter
- write sales copy for webinar
- follow up with three past clients
- spend thirty minutes on Facebook

Tuesday:

- one-hour walk
- grocery shopping
- spend thirty minutes on LinkedIn
- work on new opt-in gift for homepage
- research opportunities for speaking engagements
- finish presentation for Thursday morning

Wednesday:

- one-hour walk
- pay property taxes
- final prep for webinar
- print handouts for Thursday morning
- apply to speak to at least three conferences in 2015

Next Step: Add Your To-do List to Your Calendar

The other reason that to-do lists don't work is that they are not connected to your calendar. For creative entrepreneurs, it may feel like a stretch to do this much organization or planning. I promise that if you make planning a habit, it will create the change you want to see in your business or in your life.

The first step in using a calendar effectively is to find the type of calendar that works best for you: digital or paper? Pick the one that works best for you. I tried using both digital and paper, but that didn't work. I found that I was keeping up with all my appointments on Google calendar and not getting to my big six. I was writing them on a paper calendar but didn't always remember to check what I had written down. I would fill my calendar up with appointments, phone calls, and kids' activities, failing to schedule time to get the work done that would move me forward in my business—like marketing myself!

Block out your marketing time on your calendar first! That way you won't fill your day with other activities and leave yourself with little time or energy to complete your marketing tactics. There is no right or wrong system; just pick one and stick with it.

If you choose to work with a paper calendar, make sure you have a day-to-day calendar with plenty of space for writing. I also like the month-at-a-glance in the same calendar as well so that you can see upcoming events or programs.

For either a digital or a paper calendar, use color to organize your to-dos. I had one friend who put green around any time that was spent making money. She was a coach, so all her client meetings were green. As entrepreneurs, we have lots of hours in the day that don't generate immediate income. We don't get paid by the hour, and we don't get paid to plan, organize, or market ourselves.

Adding color as an organizing tool is a great way to make keeping your calendar more fun, and you can also track the trends of how you are spending your time. I had one member of my sales team whose calendar was inspirational! She had every day organized by the hour and everything color-coded according to the type of task: work, home, kids, sales, etc. At a glance, she knew what was coming.

Too much work and not enough play make Jane a dull girl. Too much play and not enough work make Jane a poor girl. Finding your balance between work and play will be an ongoing process. Use your calendar as a guiding light, not as a rigid structure. Notice at the end of each week how much you were able to accomplish. I'm still a fan of using gold stars, checking off tasks when they are complete, or other forms of celebrating ourselves. We always have so much to do that we rarely take a moment to celebrate how much we do get done.

Here's a silly example: I was working on the draft of this book and realized I had only about an hour before my next coaching client showed up at my front door. I had taken a one-hour walk with my husband in the morning and hadn't showered or brushed my teeth. I went upstairs to shower and realized that the bathroom counter needed a good cleaning. I had been so focused on writing that I had definitely let some of my housekeeping duties slip. I quickly took everything off the counter, found some cleaner from under the sink, and sprayed the countertop, sinks, and faucets while the shower warmed up. I jumped in the shower and when I got out, finished the cleaning. Cleaning the bathroom wasn't on my to-do list, but it needed to get done. I felt such a sense of accomplishment and relief—nothing is worse to me than a dirty bathroom. I went back to writing and working with my client, feeling refreshed and clean on several levels.

I share this to show you that you will get more things done by not overflowing your to-do list. I didn't wait until the last ten minutes to shower. I allowed myself the freedom and flexibility to take five extra minutes to do an unexpected task because I wasn't rushing. Allow the flow of the day to carry you while still committing to your big six.

Time Blocking Will Become Your Best Friend

Time blocking is one of the best time-management tips I have implemented in my business. When I don't do this, I can see where it impacts not only my work-life balance but also my bottom line. I'm just like you—if I don't plan for and commit to my marketing activities, they don't get done on a regular basis. What happens when I'm not marketing? No new clients are flowing in!

Time blocking your calendar means putting your big six into specific blocks of times dedicated to the different activities you are committed to accomplishing. In the illustration below, you can see a sample of how I have put my big six listed above into a daily calendar format.

Sample Weekly Marketing Calendar

Time	Sunday	Monday	Tuesday	Wednesday	Thursday	Friday	Saturday
7:00					Leads Networking Presentation		
8:00		Walk	Walk	Gym		Clients	
9:00		Put dinner in crockpot	Finish presentation	Property Taxes due			
10:00			Clients	Clients	Clients	Strategy sessions	
11:00		Newsletter copy	LinkedIn	Final prep for webinar and print hand-outs			
12:00		Sales copy, client follow up, Facebook	Opt-In Ideas?			Webinar	
1:00			Research	Clients	Clients		
2:00		Training call	Groceries/Carpool	Training call		Carpool	
3:00				Fill out speaking apps for 3 events		Next week's calendar prep	
4:00			Strategy sessions		Strategy sessions		
5:00		Yoga with Maggie				Walk	
6:00							
7:00							

But what about going with the flow? Being flexible? I can just hear my intuitive, creative clients grumbling about structure, so make it okay to make changes in your calendar and shift tasks around. You might create a one-hour block that says simply "marketing." You commit to spend that one hour doing one of the marketing activities on your Color Wheel Marketing Plan™, but you don't need to determine ahead of time exactly which one, especially if there are no deadlines attached.

In this first part of the chapter, I focused mainly on your daily calendar and planning. I will share with you exactly how to turn your Color Wheel Marketing Plan™ into a calendar so that it can be added to your time blocks, but first I want to share a few more tips on productivity. Most of the clients I work with work from home. This can be both a gift and a curse. If you're feeling overwhelmed and out of time, chances are it's because your space at home is not conducive to getting things done.

Challenges of Working from Home and What to Do about It

Temptations, distractions, and "make do" workspaces aren't exactly conducive to getting things done, yet that's exactly what those of us who work at home deal with every day. When I first started my publishing company in 2002, my kids were three and one. My little one was home all the time with me. My office was my dining room, which did not have doors, privacy, or any way to escape the chaos of two young children.

There are dozens of strategies and principles that claim to help you take control of your time and accomplish more than you realized was possible in a day. The question is, which ones really work? Well, of course I think that my big-six strategy and time blocking are essential to increasing productivity, but here are a few more tips that have worked for creative women entrepreneurs who work at home.

1. Mindfulness matters. Before doing a single task— breathe.

When you sit down at your desk in the morning, don't immediately start opening programs and files. Press your lower back as far back into the seat as it will go, straighten your shoulders, and take a few deep, slow breaths. Inhale through your nose and exhale through your mouth.

Then smile. Say something encouraging or complimentary to yourself.

Now you're ready to begin.

2. Make time for planning at the beginning and end of your day.

Get into the habit of taking ten minutes to go over your plans for the day (and make any necessary adjustments or add a task you've belatedly realized you still have to do) in the morning. (Make it part of sitting down at your desk with a cup of coffee.)

Last, before signing off at night, start your big-six list (containing at least your top three priorities) for the next day. (This is the list you review and add to in the mornings.)

Mindfulness Tip: These types of rituals can create boundaries and set powerful intentions for your workday, keeping you focused and on purpose. Add your daily money-tracking sheet to your end-of-day ritual. When you have completed your goals and tracking, take another deep breath, congratulate yourself for what you accomplished, state one person you are grateful for, and then walk away from work.

3. Do it now. There's nothing stopping you.

If a task is simple and quick, such as phoning to confirm an appointment, do it the moment you think of it.

In *Getting Things Done*, productivity master David Allen recommends adopting a two-minute rule: if a thing crosses your desk and can be done in two minutes or less, do it. Your time allotment might be a bit different (five or ten minutes rather than two, for example), but the principle is sound and will help keep minor tasks from clogging your to-do list.

This is part of a successful big-six routine, allowing for time to complete these unexpected tasks.

4. Organize your office.

If you chronically procrastinate or scramble to meet deadlines, it's quite likely your work area and surfaces have grown a little out of control. In fact, you may even have developed "blind spots" about chaos.

Resist the urge to tell yourself you "work best in chaos." Creative entrepreneurs are particularly prone to chaotic work environments. Who wants to organize?

Can't we just create? Take a break in the latter half of the morning or midafternoon and reorganize your physical workspace. Hint: Do this every day, and not only will it give your brain and body a refresher, your tidying will take only a few minutes.

If you decide you need a full-scale office overhaul, decide what to prioritize by answering the following questions.

- What are you always looking for on your desk?
- What never gets done? Why?
- What do you always forget? (e.g., "Where is my tax file?")
- What do you need at hand so that you can grab it without getting up?
- What can be put in your "reference" section across the room?
- What can be kicked out of your office altogether?
- What would make your office feel like a rewarding space to hang out in? (e.g., fresh flowers every week or a frame with multiple photo spots for all your kids' individual photos instead of those five awkward frames cluttering up your work area)
- What do you need in your workspace that you don't have? (e.g., a more comfortable chair, a door, a thesaurus, your own mug)

Don't get so carried away with this that it becomes your pet procrastination strategy, but do take at least two or three sessions to create your dream workspace.

5. Get a door.

If your "office" seems to be in the center of Grand Central Station, consider moving it or renovating to give yourself a door (and a wall to put the latter in, if you need it).

If you can't create or take over a separate room, invest in a nice, decorative screen (or an office cubicle screen you can pin notes on!). People psychologically are less likely to attempt to draw you into conversation if you're out of their line of sight.

One of my clients was having a hard time getting her family to respect her workspace, plus she was spending way too many late-night hours in the office. I suggested she invite her daughter, who loved to draw, to create a sign for her office door (or screen, curtain, whatever) that said "Open" or "Do not disturb" on one side and "Closed" on the reverse side. This way, her family knew when they could come in and when not to disturb her work. Plus, it shifted her mindset to turn over the "Closed" sign and walk away from her office.

It's an important mindset shift for you and your family when you work from home to create boundaries around time and space, which leads to my sixth tip for how to get more done in less time.

6. Set your work hours.

You're running a business, right? Then you need business hours. Even if those hours change to allow for kids' activities and grocery shopping and laundry day, you should make it a point to have set working hours.

Here's why: If you set your work hours ahead of your day, you can plan to fit work-related activities (and breaks) into these hours. Knowing that you "have" to be finished by 4 p.m. (or whatever "closing" time you set) can sometimes help you stay focused on getting things done. This becomes much easier to do when you use the time-blocking method of scheduling your time.

Now that I have two teens, I love working from home again and being here every day when they arrive. I work hard and put in a lot of hours because I love what I do, but when I walk out of the office, I'm done!

Chapter 14

Creating Your Marketing Calendar

Now that I have shared a few tips on how to manage your time and your space on a daily basis, I would like to turn our conversation back to some big-picture planning: your marketing calendar.

A marketing calendar is like a timeline that shows all the different products or services you might be promoting during a specific period of time and the marketing strategies you will implement to promote them.

For example, I have a client who wants to start doing monthly workshops. Filling a workshop each month will require:

1. Knowing all the dates in advance

2. Knowing where she will host at least the first one or two events

3. Knowing exactly how many people she can accommodate at each event

4. Determining what specific problems the workshops will solve for her ideal clients

5. Figuring out the best strategies for attracting that audience and spreading the word

6. Putting those strategies into a timeline format

7. Breaking each strategy down into simple steps

8. Adding those simple steps to a daily calendar to ensure they get done

Other than knowing the dates and creating a timeline, most of the information for a marketing calendar will come directly from her Color Wheel Marketing Plan™. She already knows who her ideal client is, she knows what problems she solves, and she has an idea of the best strategies for connecting with her specific audience. Now she just needs to organize her time to focus on getting the word out.

Her challenge is that she wants to spend all her time focusing on the content, design, and creation of the workshops. I keep telling her that she doesn't need to create the content until she is sure people will show up! Marketing is the most important element of business and planning. A well-executed marketing calendar ensures that the right people show up and her workshops will be full, month after month.

Perhaps you are an artist and you want to sell a certain number of paintings each month, or you are jeweler hoping to sell so many pieces each week. Your marketing calendar will include ongoing strategies for promoting and selling your work. You will need to look at your visual business plan and your Color Wheel Marketing Plan™. What is your bold money goal? How many paintings, earrings, books, etc. will you need to sell to meet your bold money goal? To whom are you selling? What problems does your product solve for them?

I worked with a client last year who sells Premier Jewelry, a network marketing company. This was Joya's first attempt at building her own business. Inside network marketing are generally two different avenues to pursue to make money: selling the jewelry directly (usually through home parties) or building a team of other people all selling the jewelry, too. The first strategy, selling jewelry through home parties, was the quickest way to get cash flowing in the door.

One of Joya's challenges was figuring out to whom she was selling jewelry and what problem the jewelry was solving for them. We worked together to create a message targeting working women who want to look professional but who also still want to be able to express their personal style with jewelry. Once we figured out the *who* and *how*, Joya could educate them on creating a more professional look, and it was easy to create a marketing message targeting her ideal clients.

Once we knew the *who* and the *how*, we could figure out which strategies would be most effective for getting Joya in front of her specific audience. We also determined how many parties Joya would need to host each week in order to meet her financial goals. Knowing the number parties she needed to host helped us determine how much marketing she would need to do.

Are you beginning to get the picture? All the work you have done so far in this book has prepared you to create an effective and actionable marketing calendar. In most companies, they are planning their marketing a year at a time. As a creative entrepreneur, I would encourage you to do your planning a quarter at a time or even on a monthly basis. You should take advantage of the flexibility and freedom you have to course correct.

Obviously, if you have some bigger projects in mind like writing a book or launching a website, you will need to create a longer-term plan. The secret to success will be chunking it down into simple steps that are easy to implement one at a time. Start with the end goal in mind and work your way backwards.

Hooray for Sticky Notes! Your Visual Marketing Action Plan

So far, you have created a one-page business plan and a Color Wheel Marketing Plan™. By now, you understand how much money you want to make, who you are targeting, and what problems you solve for them. You have a sense of the strategies you will use to attract more clients into your business. A marketing calendar will give you a big-picture view of what strategies you want to implement when, and how to break each marketing action down into manageable steps that you can add to your daily big six.

I want to share a fun, creative process for creating a quarterly marketing campaign. You could do this using a white board, poster board, or large sheets of drawing paper. You want to be able to create a calendar for three months. Why three months?

- It's hard to create consistency and momentum with most marketing strategies in fewer than ninety days.
- It trains your brain to start thinking ahead about what you could be creating instead of thinking, "Oh, crap! I need to get something out tomorrow!"
- Longer plans can feel overwhelming and not grounded in reality.

- Following your plan consistently will help you cultivate a healthy habit of implementing marketing tactics daily.

Supplies Needed:

- White board and dry-erase markers, poster board or large sheets of paper
- Ruler or yard stick
- Pencil, pen, or colored markers
- Sticky notes in three different colors

Is Your Website Attractive?

Go take a look at www.Post-it.com. Their website is beautiful. Please notice how their blog articles target their specific audience and solve problems while still showcasing their awesome products. Is your website attractive to your ideal clients? Take out your journal and brainstorm any changes you would like to make to your website to make it more attractive to your ideal client.

First, draw your ninety-day calendar on either the white board, poster or large sheet of paper. Make each square large enough to hold a sticky note. (I suggest you buy your sticky notes first.) Remember the secondary colors: orange, green, and purple? You will want one set of sticky notes to represent each of these three types of marketing strategies. They do not have to match these colors. Feel free to have fun with the colors; just make sure you have three distinct colors.

Once you have created your calendar, write down any special events, product launches, webinars, workshops, or classes that you already have planned in the next three months. If you don't have any scheduled, I suggest you go back to your Color Wheel Marketing Plan™ and look at your chosen tactics. What could you start in the next ninety days? What new offer could you make?

I would also include any weekly marketing activities you are already doing, such as your e-mail newsletter, blog post, or your weekly networking meetings. But include only activities directly related to lead generation on this particular calendar.

Now let's have some fun with planning! You will have one set of sticky notes for your referral strategies (orange), another for your in-person marketing strategies (purple), and a third set for your online strategies (green). Take a look at your Color Wheel Marketing Plan™ as well as what you have already written on the calendar. For this next layer of planning, write one marketing tactic on one sticky note. If the tactic feels big, write down one step per sticky note.

I am currently working with Julie, the graphic designer, to help her launch an e-mail newsletter as a marketing strategy. Here are all the steps she needs to take to get set up to launch this marketing tactic. Each step would become one of her big six on her daily calendar:

1. Research providers like GetResponse.com, MailChimp.com, and ConstantContact.com.

2. Pick one and sign up.

3. Add current e-mail contacts to new system.

4. Create a newsletter template.

5. Brainstorm content for next three newsletters. (Julie will send her newsletter out monthly.)

6. Schedule newsletters on her calendar.

7. Create first newsletter and schedule it to be sent out.

We will also create a juicy, attractive opt-in gift for Julie's website to encourage people to sign up for her newsletter so that she can build her list and have more people to market to. To do this, she needs to:

1. Set a deadline for when she will have the gift created. Ideas for opt-in gifts include e-books, video sources, or audio recordings.

2. Brainstorm ideas for content based on who her client is and what problem she solves for them.

3. Create the content.

4. Using GetResponse.com, create an opt-in box for her website so that when people sign up for her free gift, they are automatically added to her e-mail list.

5. Add opt-in box to her website.

6. Create a thank-you e-mail with a link to where people can download their gift.

7. Create a "Thank You" page on her website where people will be able to download, watch, or listen to the free resource Julie created.

8. Optional: create an autoresponder series to offer something else to the people who sign up, perhaps a paid report or video training series.

When we started talking about creating an e-mail newsletter to connect with her current clients and to reach out to new ones, Julie felt overwhelmed. She didn't understand the technology, and she wasn't sure she saw the value. She also had no idea what she would write about. Once we broke down the steps one by one, the process no longer felt overwhelming.

When Julie realized that she was writing content that would help her clients, she knew exactly what she wanted to write about. Also, when you use an e-newsletter system like GetResponse.com, you create a template once and just drop in new content each time. Most of the process becomes automated and simplified. Julie doesn't have to send the free gift to everyone that signs up; the system does this for her. This is a great example of how systems can liberate you.

Once you have completed your big-picture calendar, you will know exactly what you need to do every single day to market your business. Transfer the information on your visual calendar to you daily calendar, making each step in the process one of your big six on a daily basis.

This may seem like an extra step, but if you don't put your marketing activities into the calendar you use every day, you will fill up your time with other activities and not get to marketing. Marketing makes you money, and making money is why you are in business, right? Yes, I know you have other altruistic motives, but remember that learning to love your money will help you be a better marketer. The truth is that increasing the money you make, increases the capacity you have to serve more people!

How Much Marketing Do I Need to Do?

I hear this question over and over again from my clients. The simple answer? A minimum of thirty minutes a day should be dedicated to marketing activities. The truth? It depends on how many clients you are trying to attract, how many clients you have right now, and how good you are at sales.

If you are new in business and are just starting to market yourself and your products and services, chances are you need to spend as much as 90 percent of your time on marketing until you reach your monthly financial goals.

If you are doing well but you are ready to take your business to the next level, determine how many new clients or new sales you need per week. How will you find those clients? Where are they spending their time? What will be the most effective way to connect with them?

Decide which tactics you want to use and start adding them one or two at a time to your master marketing calendar. Don't try to add ten new tactics to your marketing calendar all at once. Take your time, master one, and create systems to automate as much of your marketing as possible.

Chapter 15

Supporting the Creative Entrepreneur: A Spouse's Perspective

Note from Minette: In this chapter you will find insights, advice and reflections written by my husband Brad Dobson. If you are a creative entrepreneur who is married, share this chapter with your spouse. It might help them to understand how you work but it will also help you to see why they appear to be frustrated and unsupportive of your ideas at times.

As a family we've always been fortunate that my career and salary were enough to support us. It's given us the opportunity to enable Minette to focus on trying to take her ideas to fruition and build a business out of it. I'm also a creative type—I enjoy music, software, and writing—so I know all too well the need to fulfill that drive.

I'm less of an entrepreneur than she is, and my software day job provides me a creative outlet at least some of the time. As our kids have grown up, I took the role of provider so that Minette could take some risks and be flexible for the kids.

That said, sometimes it is a struggle to have a job, keep being supportive, and understand what a strange beast the creative entrepreneur can be. It can be a challenge to know how to help ramp up their business enterprise in a sane fashion.

"Oh no, not again. Why can't she just focus?"

"Seems like every times he starts to get traction with one thing there's a new idea, new domain name, new website."

"This would be a lot easier if she just got a job and felt the satisfaction of a regular paycheck, but it's hard to see so much creativity forced into a nine-to-five box."

I can't count the number of different ideas my wife has floated by me on her entrepreneurial journey—without trying to define what she wanted to do with any precision. It would go something like this: "I bought this online course, and I have a new idea that sounds great. Others are making tons doing this. Let's buy a new domain, set up a new WordPress site, and buy a new plugin for affiliate marketing. I'll switch my old blog to be just for my art and personal stuff." Arrggh! Just say no.

Many times I've interpreted this as another attempt to get rich quick. In reality it's a combination of things: a lack of a clear professional identity; the bright, shiny object syndrome (as Minette described earlier in the book); and a lack of systems, which leads to wanting to find a quick way to grow instead of building on incremental successes.

The bright, shiny object syndrome isn't necessarily a bad thing. In fact, a huge part of being a creative person is to get excited about new ideas. The lack of identity and business systems create bigger problems and can leave the creative entrepreneur feeling rudderless. Below are some of the things I have learned along the way. I'm not always good at following my own advice, but I hope they will help you in your journey as either a creative entrepreneur or a confused spouse.

What do you want to be when you grow up?

This does not appear to be a question that many creative entrepreneurs have ever answered clearly. Help them find their professional identity as soon as possible. It will certainly change as time goes on—whose doesn't?—but you both need that identity to be able to frame the conversation.

A friend of mine asked me once, "What does your wife do for a living?" and I couldn't give him a good answer. It turns out neither could my wife. Can you answer that question about your significant other?

It strengthens your relationship to know their professional identity even (especially!) if their business is in an amorphous start-up phase. This aligns closely to the earlier chapters in the book detailing how the creative entrepreneur needs to identify the problems they solve and their ideal client. Their spouse will struggle with seeing them as a business owner if they don't have a clear professional identity.

Some creative entrepreneurs have already figured this out when they start their business. Maybe they are one of the lucky few who can simply open an Etsy store and have people buy their products. If they are not clear, my suggestion is to get this done now. Here are some questions you might ask. Be direct but loving: this is about bringing a dose of reality to the situation.

"Where do you see this business in six months? one year? two years?"

"Why exactly are you in business? What do you hope to achieve?"

"Are you prepared to be in front of people to market your business and sell your products?"

"Do you understand that in order to grow, this has to be more than just a hobby business creating art?"

"What are your sales projections for the next two months?"

"What specific things will you do to make or exceed those projections and keep growing this business?" Hint: the answer isn't "Make more art."

Financial Dollars and Sense

I am lazy about my finances, but as a creative type, my wife avoids them if left unsupervised. She is getting better, but helping her with money is important. Creative entrepreneurs want to make their art and not worry about finances. You need to take extra steps to make those things go smoothly.

How they will manage their finances will depend on the size of your spouse's business, but here are some ways to support them:

- Get personal systems in place to isolate their business income and spending such as a separate checking account and a single, separate credit card for their business.
- Set up something like QuickBooks online that is relatively easy and your accountant can work with easily.
- Spend extra for professionals such as CPAs and tax people.
- Show your spouse their income and spending with trends and graphs, not numbers. They are visual people.
- Set up a financial date with your spouse maybe bi-weekly. Make it feel professional at a coffee shop

rather than with a glass of wine and the TV on. Just talk about what's happening in their business finances, and for thirty minutes max.

Engaging your spouse and actively helping them with their business finances (or paying professionals when you know it's not something you can handle) will save money and stress, but it will also help them focus on being an entrepreneur and not just being creative.

Helping with other business systems

The marketing planning that Minette details in this book is a great example of a system that the creative entrepreneur can use to keep on track as their spouse tries to assist them in setting up and maintaining their own business systems that alleviate day-to-day stresses. Don't let them blow off the networking meeting because they are in another creative tizzy. Mend the tent so that it goes up easily at the art show. Help set up the tripod and lights for recording a YouTube video. Help with setting up and maintaining technology so that the money can flow in smoothly.

The list never ends, and you can quickly be buried by it while working your own full-time job. When it gets too much or when there are things that neither of you have the skillset to do, insist on hiring service people to keep the systems going. I'm not talking about full-time employees; I'm talking about services. A virtual assistant that can handle the online presence, a travel agent, a CPA, an online financial system like QuickBooks Online, and a simple way to take credit card payments are all business systems that can ease stress. Do they cost more? Sure. But wouldn't you rather have your weekends off?

Adding one good business habit at a time

I've been on a personal journey lately to try and bring better personal habits into my life and undo more than forty years of ineffective and self-destructive conditioning. I'm adding things like "twenty minutes of meditation per day," "no eating after dinner," and "make the bed every morning." These are examples of simple mindfulness patterns. I use an iOS app called "Way of Life" that helps me track things daily and brings extra visibility to how I am progressing.

After I feel a new behavior has become habitual, I add something new to the app. Each new habit usually that takes a few weeks to cement. It is both freeing and scary to add only one thing at a time: freeing because I can focus on just one thing, scary because I have to force myself not to try and fix everything at once (which leads to inevitable overload and failure).

Could you use the same approach with your business? Can you find just one small marketing or business system to start getting good at and track it daily for two to three weeks? You'll be surprised how many things you have added after a few months *without getting stuck.*

Bring the Focus Back to the Business

There will be lots of new ideas. Try not to overreact when they are brought up. Rather, try and discuss them in the context of the professional identity we talked about earlier. Many will be just ideas and stop there; others may turn into great business opportunities down the road.

Sometimes the creative mind wanders off into fairyland on flights of fancy. That can lead to amazing beauty and insight. Your job as a partner is to ensure that those thoughts also return to the entrepreneurial part of the equation. Ask your creative spouse these questions:

"Mm hmm. How does that idea reinforce your business? How will that help you market and bring in more customers?"

"Is there a way you can do that new project and still keep your other commitments?"

"I noticed you spent the last two days making tie-dyed sweaters for our garden gnomes to make them more Christmas-ey. Nice. Do you think they'll do well on the Etsy store in a Christmas promotion?"

Always encourage their art, but make sure they don't stop marketing their business while they are being creative. Minette loves to write and will get caught up in blogging (or giant Christmas projects, or this book!). All of a sudden a week has gone by and there haven't been any speaking opportunities or one-on-one conversations courting potential clients. That missed week turns into crappy sales two months down the road. Creative entrepreneurs can recharge and refresh through their art, but they can also hide in it.

Chapter 16

Creating Accountability Is Key to the Creative Entrepreneur's Success

You made it! You're at the end of the planning stage. Now it is time to implement. You may be feeling super jazzed and excited about all your colorful new plans. You may feel ready to jump right in and start attracting more cash and clients—fast!

Then life happens, you get stuck or don't know how to do something, someone gets sick, the car dies, and on and on. As a creative entrepreneur, one of your biggest challenges will be keeping the momentum going and not getting distracted by life's craziness or the next bright, shiny idea. In chapter 14 my husband shared how easily I get distracted. I empathize with the challenge of working alone and with the challenges of being a busy working wife and mother. Staying on track has become my top priority in my business but keeping the momentum can be a challenge!

What will it take to keep the momentum going and keep you on task, focused on becoming an amazing marketer? One thing—accountability. I find that creative women entrepreneurs need someone in their life and business to hold them accountable, to be their cheerleader and their champion when they get frustrated or stuck.

Do you currently have someone like that in your life? It might be a business partner, a spouse, a girlfriend, or a business coach like me. I want to encourage you to find someone who is willing to hold you accountable while being supportive and understanding. Make sure to pick someone you feel safe with so that can share your frustrations and your dreams. Finding a local mentor in your community is another great option for creating accountability.

One of the biggest challenges of being an entrepreneur, especially if you work from home, is the isolation. At times you will feel lonely, disconnected, and perhaps even insane. It's important to surround yourself with other entrepreneurs. This is another benefit of networking and connecting with business owners who are going through the same experiences and challenges you are.

One of my most favorite forms of accountability is a mastermind group. A mastermind group can be a small group of colleagues who meet monthly or by phone to hold each other accountable and support each other through challenges. Masterminds are great for brainstorming solutions to problems and for sharing resources.

Whatever format works best for you, be sure to add "find one or more accountability partners" to your big six soon. This will ensure that all the hard work you did to create your plan will have a big payoff in the next three to six months, without you feeling lost, losing momentum, or struggling alone.

I want to congratulate you for joining me on this creative journey through mindset, money, and marketing! My hope is that you are beginning to understand the power of your mindset and that you are learning to love money and marketing. By now, you should be able to look at the plans you created and proudly proclaim: I am an artful marketer!

In Gratitude

I would be so grateful if you could take a minute or two to share what you loved about this book and provide an honest review on our Amazon sales page at http://bit.ly/artful-marketer.

About the Author

Dr. Minette Riordan successfully built a 6-figure multi-media publishing company targeting families in the Dallas/Ft. Worth Metroplex. For over 10 years she ran Scissortail Publishing, publishing a monthly magazine, a website and several annual family expos. She credits her success to learning how to connect with others through networking, referrals, strategic partnerships and an attitude of service to others first. Minette's secret to sales success is not about winning a numbers game, but playing the people game: cultivating an attitude of curiosity and openness that will quickly help you attract clients and fans.

Education

Prior to starting her company, Minette was an educator who earned her Ph.D. from Stanford University in 1995. She has a BA from Texas A&M University and an MA from the University of Texas at Austin. She has taught at the university and high school levels, as well as adult education and personal development workshops.

Certifications

Minette is a lifelong learner and holds a variety of certifications from the following organizations. She hasn't stopped studying since she got out of graduate school. As much as she loves teaching others, she loves being a student, constantly growing and evolving into the next phase of her life. She uses all of these different tools to help her clients fulfill their dreams.

- 2006 - Certified Coach for Parents - Academy for Parent Coaching International

- 2007 - CRG Licensed Facilitator – Personal Style Indicator

- 2013 - Life Optimization Coach – Life Optimization Coaching

- 2012 - SoulCollage® facilitator

- 2014 - Sacred Money Archetypes facilitator

- 2014 - Zentangle® teacher

- 2015 - ARTbundance coach

Awards

Dr. Riordan received the 2007 Altrusa Outstanding Women of Today award and was named the 2009 Small Business Owner of the Year by the Plano Chamber of Commerce. In 2011, the Texas Home Child Care

Association honored her with the Libby Linebarger award for her commitment to education.

Media

Dr. Minette Riordan has been featured in numerous television and radio interviews on ABC, CBS, TimeWarner and Fox Radio. She also hosted her own radio show on talk radio in the Dallas area.

Minette's Passions, Hobbies and Interests

Minette's interest in spirituality and personal development were started with a service trip to Peru when she was 15 and found herself sitting at the base of the majestic Macchu Picchu ruins. Little did she know where that journey would take her! Minette's passions include spiritual growth, art, creative writing, poetry, gourmet cooking, collecting unusual earrings and walking on the beach near her home in Santa Barbara, CA.

Her passion and joy come from helping others find the information, tools and inspiration they need to succeed. She is living proof that you can have it all: a successful business, healthy marriage and happy kids! She would never say her journey to this point was easy and she learned a great deal about herself along the way but she is loving her life!

Minette is also a wife, mom and lover of all things crafty and creative. She has spent the last several years getting in touch with her inner artist and falling in love with making art. Remembering how to be creative has helped Minette implement dramatic and wonderful changes in her life, especially being able to release her inner critic. Creativity is infused into every aspect of her daily routine from making dinner for her family, to admiring the gorgeous area in which she lives, to writing an artful blog post or teaching workshops.

Connect with Minette Riordan, Ph.D.

Learn more about Minette and her work at:

www.minetteriordan.com

www.mindfulpatterns.com

Connect with Minette on social media:

www.facebook.com/coachminette

www.twitter.com/minetter

http://www.linkedin.com/in/minetteriordan

You read the book, now what?

A special offer for ongoing support and accountability.

You may have read every word in *The Artful Marketer* but did you take the time to do the work?

Did you create your one-page business plan and your color wheel marketing plan?

Did you write your marketing activities into your calendar?

If you are feeling both excited and overwhelmed by all the details you need to manage to grow your business, then you are in the right place!

Now is the perfect time to invest in yourself and in your business. Make this year your BEST YEAR EVER by getting the support you need!

I have helped hundreds of creative entrepreneurs just like you to build profitable businesses by creating a vibrant, visual and dynamic business strategy that works. To celebrate the launch of *The Artful Marketer* book, I have designed a brand new group coaching program to offer you the ongoing support and accountability you need to implement everything I teach in the book.

I am here to tell you that there is a better and easier way to make the money you deserve, to work smarter <u>not harder</u> and to finally create freedom and financial independence.

You don't have to do this alone!

Join The Artful Marketer's 6-Figure Breakthrough Club

Something you should know is that creating a marketing plan has helped my clients to **double and triple their income** in a very short period of time. <u>The Artful Marketer</u> book is the exact process I have used to help dozens of creative entrepreneurs achieve their financial goals. They are no longer riding the rollercoaster of feast or famine in their business and they continue to see double-digit increases in their bottom line.

If you read my book, you understand that any business model can benefit from having a **strategic marketing plan.** Once you get the formula for marketing and attracting more of your ideal clients, you can **easily accomplish** your **income** goals AND reduce how much time you work, freeing up your time and energy to pursue other business-building projects or spend more time with family?

Are you...

- ☑ Needing to generate cash right now and don't know what marketing will work for you?

- ☑ Investing in marketing tactics that aren't generating any leads or generating the wrong leads?

- ☑ Speaking and networking but not connecting with the right people?

- ☑ Frustrated by not knowing how to create a plan that will work for you and your business?

- ☑ Overwhelmed, over-worked and over-tired from trying to be everything for everyone?

- ☑ Secretly feeling envious of the success you see other people having and wondering what you are doing wrong?

- ☑ Feeling stuck at the same income level as

last year and year the before?

 Wanting to get the next level of financial success in your business but have no clue how you will find the time or what steps to take?

Let's be honest, the joy of being a creative entrepreneur fades fast when you're trying to generate necessary cash flow and you're short on time, either because you're new and you need to get money rolling in to grow your business...or you're a seasoned entrepreneur and you need to do something — fast, to free up your time and give yourself breathing room so you can focus on taking your business to the next level.

Cash flow is the lifeblood of every business and creating enough of it is a serious problem that creative entrepreneurs need to solve ... TODAY!

Which is WHY creating a marketing plan is my **FAVORITE** answer to solving these problems. I'm delighted to announce the debut of my brand new **Artful Marketer's 6-Figure Breakthrough** coaching program, in which I teach YOU my **simple**, tried and true formula for creating and implementing your own insanely **profitable** Artful Marketing Plan — **saving** you from spending your limited time trying to figure it out all by yourself, and making it quick and simple for you to get into action and start smoothing out that money rollercoaster now.

Every time I mention that I can help creative entrepreneurs master the art of marketing their business in 30 minutes a day or less in my workshops, training or coaching programs people clamor to find out all the how-to details. Which is why, after years of helping my clients create their perfect marketing plans, **I knew it was time to share my Artful Marketing Plan secrets with more people and I wanted to make it affordable, accessible and super creative.**

Get excited, because this group coaching program is so dynamic, you'll quickly find yourself:

- **passionate** about your business again,
- **implementing** your plan daily, without stretching your time or your budget,
- **generating** more of the right leads than you ever thought possible,
- **having** more time to spend doing the work you love, and
- **celebrating** your new financial success.

The **Artful Marketing 6-Figure Breakthrough Club** will help you to streamline your business so that you have more time, less stress and are making more profit than you dreamed was possible! And you get all of that plus the ongoing support of a loving, artful and like-minded community of creative entrepreneurs.

This 12-month group coaching program is perfect for you if you have been struggling to grow your business on your own.

This is the perfect program for you, and I'm ready to walk you through exactly how, step by step...

When I first started coaching and consulting I **mistakenly thought** I didn't need the fancy marketing strategy and business planning that I used to build my 6-figure publishing company. Wow, was I wrong.

I really floundered my first year in business, even though I knew that planning was what I needed. Once I sat down, put a plan in place and implemented my plan – I tripled my income! Planning works.

Don't make the same mistake I did! In this 12-month group coaching program, you will discover the simple structure to create an effective marketing plan with step by step instruction, templates and handouts so that you can focus on what works.

Once I realized that I could use my **artistic gifts and talents** to create **a marketing plan that works**, I was so excited. I **mistakenly believed** that I had to create a traditional business and marketing plan based on spreadsheets and analytics.

And now I'm going to teach you how to do the same plus I will provide you with the accountability you need to create sustainable success all year long.

Here's exactly what you can expect:

- 21-Day Quick Start Guide to jumpstart your marketing
- Access to Minette's extensive library of marketing audios, checklists, and templates
- One live marketing webinar each month on a particular aspect of mindset, money or marketing
- One Q&A call each month where you can ask Minette anything and get one-one live coaching
- Private Facebook group for ongoing support, sharing and networking
- Weekly email tips and motivation to keep you on track
- Weekly ARTsignments® and Mindfulness tips
- A fun combination of the practical, the playful and the profitable

The value of this program is well over $1,000.00. I am so committed to your success, that I want to make this easy for you to say yes! Just for readers of <u>The Artful Marketer</u> book, I am offering a $200 discount on this 12-month program!

Use the discount code: ArtfulMarketer to receive your discount today. You can find more details and register at: http://www.mindfulpatterns.com/6-figure-club

Here's what Minette's clients have to say:

"A super big thank you to Minette Riordan for being an AMAZING, AMAZING coach and for bringing me back to life. In less then one month she has already helped me turn the tables and start to rock my graphic design business again! She is brilliant with her input, advice, strategies, ideas, support and guidance and really wants to help you succeed."

- Brittany Allen, 2nd Story Design

One month working with <u>Minette Riordan</u> and my sales have doubled!!! She has helped me grow my business quicker and bigger than I could have imagined. My investment in her is the best investment with the biggest payoff that I have ever made for my business.

– Stephanie Grisham, Grisham Farms

"Before our session I felt stuck and unclear, now I am clear about what I'm offering, who I'm offering it to, and have an easy to follow plan of action. You had such an incredible ability to use creative and fun tools to help me focus in on what my ideal client looks like...thanks again and I look forward to working with you again!"

- Ellany Cevan

"Minette's clear insight and feedback reignites my passion for my purpose. In our conversation, Minette brilliantly guided me to the core of what I want to do next in my business. She masterfully asked questions so I uncovered my perfect niche and helped me translate my ideas into a tangible benefit for my ideal client."

- Kathy Garland, Kathy Garland International

"Minette, I can't thank you enough for the value you brought to me for my company. You helped me achieve the goals I was striving for and in such a short time. With your amazing knowledge and expertise, I have grown as a business owner AND met what I was hoping for. I would recommend anyone wanting to learn more about marketing their business to connect with Minette. She is such fun to work with and has all the skills necessary to assist anyone in business. Thank you!"

- Heather Quiring, Travel Directions

Resources

Jennifer Bourn. "Color Meaning: Meaning of the Color Purple" January 5, 2011.
http://www.bourncreative.com/meaning-of-the-color-purple/

Jennifer Bourn. "Color Meaning: Meaning of the Color Red" February 25, 2011.
http://www.bourncreative.com/meaning-of-the-color-red/

"Common Links Among Visual Learners"
http://www.time4learning.com/visual-learners.shtml

Maeve Duggan and Aaron Smith "Social Media Update 2013" Pew Research Internet Project. December 30, 2013. http://www.pewinternet.org/2013/12/30/social-media-update-2013/

Ryan Eliason. The 10 Best Ways to Get Paid for Changing the World. E-book Copyright 2014, p. 61.
http://www.the10bestways.com

Marney Madrikakis. Founder of Artellaland and the ARTbundance coaching program.
http://www.artellaland.com

Linda Naiman. "What is creativity?" Feb. 17, 2014
http://www.creativityatwork.com/2014/02/17/what-is-creativity/

Judy Scott-Kemmis. "The Color Blue"
http://www.empower-yourself-with-color-psychology.com/color-blue.html

Judy Scott-Kemmis. "The Color Yellow"
http://www.empower-yourself-with-color-psychology.com/color-yellow.html

Kendall Summerhawk. Sacred Money
Archetypes®. http://www.kendallsummerhawk.com/moneyarchetypes/

Twyla Tharp, *The Creative Habit*: *Learn It and Use It for Life* (©2003 W.A.T. Ltd. (P)2013 Audible, Inc.)

"What is mindfulness?"
http://greatergood.berkeley.edu/topic/mindfulness/definition

31063938R00150

Made in the USA
Middletown, DE
16 April 2016